The Future of Waste Management

1

Cutting-Edge Technologies and Practices for a
Sustainable Tomorrow

Oswald Dean

The Future of Waste Management

This document is geared towards providing exact and reliable information with regards to the topic and issue covered. The publication is sold with the idea that the publisher is not required to render accounting, officially permitted, or otherwise, qualified services. If advice is necessary, legal or professional, a practiced individual in the profession should be ordered.

From a Declaration of Principles which was accepted and approved equally by a Committee of the American Bar Association and a Committee of Publishers and Associations.

TABLE OF CONTENTS

Chapter 1: The Evolution of Waste Management

Historical Overview of Waste Practices

Waste management, a concept deeply intertwined with human civilization, has evolved significantly over centuries. Tracing its roots, one discovers a tale not just of refuse but of human adaptation, innovation, and the relentless pursuit of better living conditions. The history of waste practices offers a window into societal values, technological advancements, and environmental consciousness.

In ancient times, waste management was rudimentary. Early humans, living as nomads, left behind waste that was primarily organic and decomposable. The impact was minimal, given the sparse population and the biodegradable nature of their refuse. However, as societies began to settle and grow into organized communities, the challenge of waste management emerged. The earliest known waste management system can be traced back to the Minoan civilization on the island of Crete, around 3000 BCE. Here, waste was systematically collected and moved away from living areas, a practice that laid the groundwork for future waste management strategies.

With the rise of urbanization, the challenges of waste management intensified. Ancient Rome, a bustling metropolis of its time, developed a sophisticated system to manage its waste. The Romans constructed aqueducts and sewer systems, such as the Cloaca Maxima, one of the world's earliest sewage systems. This infrastructure not only transported waste away from the city but also demonstrated an understanding of the public health hazards posed by unmanaged waste. Roman waste collectors, known as 'coprologists,' were tasked with removing waste from homes and streets, highlighting an early form of public waste management service.

The Middle Ages, however, saw a regression in waste management practices. As the Roman Empire fell, so did its advanced systems. Europe was plagued by unsanitary conditions, with waste often discarded in the streets, leading to public health crises like the Black Death. It was a period marked by neglect and a lack of innovation in waste management, reflecting broader societal challenges.

The Industrial Revolution in the 18th and 19th centuries marked a turning point. Rapid urbanization and industrialization led to unprecedented waste generation. Cities swelled with migrants seeking employment, and the volume of waste, now including industrial byproducts, skyrocketed. The need for organized waste management became critical. In response, the late 19th century saw major cities like London and Paris develop structured waste collection systems. The introduction of waste incineration plants, or "destructors," in the UK marked a pivotal moment. These facilities aimed to reduce the volume of waste through combustion, reflecting a shift towards more systematic waste management approaches.

Simultaneously, the concept of recycling began to take root. The "rag and bone" men of Victorian England collected discarded items for resale or repurposing, an early form of recycling. This period also saw the establishment of waste management as a formalized public service, with municipalities taking on the responsibility of waste collection and disposal.

The 20th century brought further advancements. The rise of environmental awareness, spurred by events like the publication of Rachel Carson's "Silent Spring" in 1962, led to a reevaluation of waste management practices. The environmental movement of the 1960s and 1970s catalyzed the development of more sustainable waste management strategies. This era saw the introduction of sanitary landfills, designed to minimize environmental impact by containing waste and reducing leachate emissions. The implementation of these landfills marked a significant improvement over open dumping, highlighting a growing commitment to environmental stewardship.

The latter half of the 20th century also witnessed the establishment of recycling programs as a mainstream waste management strategy. The first Earth Day in 1970 and the subsequent establishment of the Environmental Protection Agency (EPA) in the United States underscored the importance of recycling. Municipal recycling programs became widespread, encouraging the separation and collection of recyclable materials such as paper, glass, and metals. These efforts were bolstered by public education campaigns aimed at raising awareness about the benefits of recycling.

This period also saw the rise of waste-to-energy initiatives, which sought to convert waste into usable energy forms. Incineration plants were equipped with energy recovery systems, allowing them to generate electricity or heat from waste combustion. This approach not only reduced waste volume but also provided an alternative energy source, aligning with broader goals of resource conservation and energy diversification.

Entering the 21st century, waste management continues to evolve, driven by technological innovation, regulatory frameworks, and heightened environmental consciousness. The concept of zero waste, which aims to minimize waste generation through comprehensive recycling and reuse strategies, has gained traction. Cities across the globe have set ambitious targets to reduce landfill dependency and embrace circular economy principles, wherein waste is viewed as a resource rather than a burden.

Modern waste management practices are increasingly characterized by the integration of advanced technologies. Smart waste management systems, leveraging data analytics and digital platforms, optimize waste collection routes, monitor landfill conditions, and enhance resource recovery processes. These innovations reflect a shift towards more efficient and data-driven waste management solutions.

The historical journey of waste practices is a testament to human ingenuity and resilience. From the rudimentary systems of ancient civilizations to the sophisticated, technology-driven approaches of today, waste management has continually adapted to meet the challenges of its time. This evolution underscores a fundamental truth: as societies grow and change, so too must the strategies we employ to manage the byproducts of our existence. In this ongoing journey, the lessons of the past serve as a guiding light, illuminating the path towards a more sustainable and harmonious future.

Milestones in Waste Management Innovation

Throughout history, the quest to manage waste effectively has been marked by significant innovations. Each milestone reflects a step forward in addressing the challenges posed by waste, showcasing human ingenuity in turning potential liabilities into opportunities.

The late 19th century marked a pivotal shift as the Industrial Revolution brought about unprecedented urban growth and industrial output. This period saw the introduction of the first refuse incinerators in the UK, known as "destructors." These facilities aimed to tackle the mounting waste volumes by incinerating refuse to reduce its mass. Although rudimentary by today's standards, destructors represented a critical leap toward systematic waste management, establishing incineration as a viable method for waste reduction.

The early 20th century witnessed the development of sanitary landfills, a significant advancement over open dumping practices. The concept involved burying waste in a methodical manner, covering it with soil to minimize exposure to the environment. This approach aimed to control odor, reduce pest infestation, and prevent the spread of diseases. Sanitary landfills demonstrated an evolving understanding of environmental protection and public health, setting the stage for more sophisticated waste disposal methods.

World War II brought challenges and innovations in resource management. During this period, recycling became a patriotic duty. Metal, rubber, and paper were collected and repurposed to support the war effort. This era underscored the value of resource recovery, embedding the principles of recycling into societal consciousness and paving the way for post-war recycling movements.

The 1960s and 1970s marked a turning point as environmental awareness took center stage. The publication of Rachel Carson's "Silent Spring" in 1962 catalyzed the modern environmental movement, driving a reevaluation of waste management practices. This era saw the emergence of recycling as a mainstream practice. Municipalities across the United States and other countries began implementing curbside recycling programs, encouraging households to separate recyclable materials from their waste. This shift not only reduced landfill dependency but also fostered a culture of environmental responsibility.

Simultaneously, the concept of waste-to-energy gained traction. Incineration plants equipped with energy recovery systems began transforming waste into electricity and heat. This innovation addressed multiple challenges: reducing waste volume, generating renewable energy, and minimizing landfill use. Waste-to-energy technology exemplified the potential of turning waste into a valuable resource, aligning with growing sustainability goals.

The late 20th century introduced the concept of hazardous waste management. The Love Canal disaster in the United States highlighted the dangers of improper waste disposal, leading to the establishment of regulations governing hazardous waste. The Comprehensive Environmental Response, Compensation, and Liability Act (CERCLA), enacted in 1980, addressed the management of hazardous waste sites, emphasizing the importance of safe disposal and environmental remediation.

As the 21st century unfolded, technological advancements began to revolutionize waste management. The rise of single-stream recycling simplified the recycling process for consumers by allowing all recyclables to be collected together. This innovation increased recycling rates and reduced contamination, making recycling more accessible and efficient.

Simultaneously, advancements in material science led to the development of biodegradable and compostable materials.

These materials, designed to break down naturally, presented solutions to the growing challenge of plastic waste. Compostable packaging and products gained popularity as environmentally conscious alternatives to traditional plastics, furthering the shift toward sustainable waste management practices.

Modern waste management is characterized by the integration of data-driven solutions. Smart waste management systems, utilizing digital technologies, optimize waste collection routes, monitor landfill conditions, and enhance resource recovery. These systems exemplify the convergence of technology and waste management, offering more efficient and sustainable solutions.

The concept of the circular economy has emerged as a transformative approach to waste management. This model seeks to minimize waste generation by designing products for reuse, repair, and recycling. It challenges the traditional linear economy of "take, make, dispose," promoting a closed-loop system where waste becomes a resource. Successful initiatives demonstrate the potential of circular practices, highlighting the economic and environmental benefits of reducing waste and maximizing resource efficiency.

In recent years, there has been a growing emphasis on collaborative efforts in waste management. Governments, businesses, and communities are joining forces to tackle global waste challenges. International agreements, such as the Basel Convention, aim to regulate the transboundary movement of hazardous waste, fostering cooperation and accountability. Collaborative initiatives underscore the interconnectedness of waste management, emphasizing the need for global solutions to address shared challenges.

Milestones in waste management innovation reflect a continuous journey toward more sustainable and efficient practices. From the early days of incineration and landfills to the modern era of recycling, waste-to-energy, and circular economy models, each advancement builds upon the lessons of the past. These innovations not only address the immediate challenges of waste management but also pave the way for a future where waste is viewed as a resource rather than a burden. As societies continue to evolve, the ingenuity and adaptability demonstrated throughout history will remain essential in shaping the waste management strategies of tomorrow.

Transitioning from Traditional to Modern Methods

The journey from traditional waste management methods to modern practices is an intricate narrative of adaptation and innovation, driven by necessity and a growing awareness of environmental impacts. Traditional methods, characterized by simple disposal techniques, have gradually given way to sophisticated systems designed to minimize waste and maximize resource recovery.

Historically, waste disposal was a straightforward affair. In rural communities, organic waste was composted or fed to livestock, while non-biodegradable materials were often buried or burned. Urban areas, however, faced greater challenges due to higher population densities and limited space. In many cities, waste was simply dumped in open pits or waterways, leading to unsanitary conditions and serious public health issues. Over time, it became clear that more systematic approaches were needed.

The shift towards modern waste management began in earnest during the late 19th and early 20th centuries, as cities grew and industrialization increased waste production. The advent of organized municipal waste collection marked the first significant transition. Cities like Paris and New York implemented regular waste collection services, transporting rubbish away from urban centers. This development underscored the importance of coordinated efforts in managing waste, highlighting a move away from individual disposal practices.

As the 20th century progressed, technological advancements facilitated further changes. The introduction of sanitary landfills, where waste is compacted and buried under layers of soil, represented a major improvement over open dumping. These landfills were designed to prevent environmental contamination and reduce health risks, reflecting a growing understanding of the need to protect natural ecosystems. Additionally, waste incineration plants emerged, offering a method to reduce waste volume through combustion, though they also introduced concerns about air pollution.

The mid-20th century saw a burgeoning environmental movement that reshaped public attitudes toward waste. Society began to recognize the finite nature of natural resources and the environmental impacts of unchecked waste generation. Recycling emerged as a key component of modern waste management, encouraged by both grassroots initiatives and government policies. The establishment of curbside recycling programs made it easier for households to participate, promoting a culture of reuse and resource conservation.

This era also saw the rise of waste-to-energy technologies. Plants capable of converting waste into electricity or heat became more common, offering a dual benefit: waste reduction and energy production. The ability to harness energy from waste aligned with broader sustainability goals, providing an alternative to fossil fuels and highlighting the potential of waste as a resource.

As environmental awareness continued to grow, the concept of waste minimization gained traction. This approach emphasizes reducing waste generation at its source through strategies such as designing products for durability, repair, and recyclability. Manufacturers began to adopt principles of eco-design, creating products that require fewer resources and generate less waste over their lifecycle. This shift reflected a deeper understanding of the interconnectedness of production, consumption, and waste, laying the groundwork for sustainable practices.

The integration of technology into waste management marked a significant advancement in the transition from traditional to modern methods. Sensor-equipped waste bins, automated sorting facilities, and advanced data analytics have transformed waste management into a more efficient and precise operation. These technologies enable real-time monitoring and optimization of waste collection and processing, reducing inefficiencies and enhancing resource recovery.

Contemporary waste management also prioritizes the principles of the circular economy, which seeks to close the loop by keeping resources in use for as long as possible. This model promotes the idea of designing out waste and pollution, keeping products and materials in use, and regenerating natural systems. Businesses and governments alike are exploring circular initiatives, from extended producer responsibility programs to innovative recycling technologies, all aimed at reducing waste and conserving resources.

The transition from traditional to modern waste management methods is not without challenges. Infrastructure development, regulatory frameworks, and public participation are critical components of successful waste management systems. Developing countries, in particular, face unique obstacles, as rapid urbanization and limited resources complicate efforts to implement modern practices. Nevertheless, international collaboration and knowledge sharing are helping to bridge these gaps, fostering a global commitment to sustainable waste management.

Public awareness and education play crucial roles in facilitating this transition. Empowering individuals with knowledge about the impacts of waste and the benefits of modern management practices encourages responsible behavior and supports systemic change. Community engagement initiatives, educational campaigns, and transparent communication are essential tools in building a culture of sustainability.

The journey from traditional waste management to modern methods is ongoing, marked by continuous innovation and adaptation. As societies strive to balance economic growth with environmental stewardship, waste management remains a critical area of focus. The evolution of waste practices reflects not only technological advancements but also a fundamental shift in societal values towards sustainability and resource conservation. In this dynamic landscape, the ability to learn from the past and embrace new solutions will be key to achieving a sustainable future.

Influence of Industrialization on Waste Generation

The advent of industrialization marked a significant turning point in human history, one that brought about profound changes in how societies functioned. Among its many impacts, industrialization dramatically influenced waste generation, altering the volume, composition, and management of waste in ways that continue to shape modern practices.

Before the Industrial Revolution, waste production was relatively modest. Communities were predominantly agrarian, and the materials they used were largely organic and biodegradable. Waste products were typically reabsorbed by the environment, posing minimal threat to the ecosystem. However, the onset of industrialization in the late 18th century initiated a period of rapid urbanization and technological advancement, fundamentally altering the waste landscape.

As industries began to proliferate, they brought with them a surge in the production of goods. This increase in manufacturing led to a corresponding rise in waste generation. Factories produced large volumes of by-products and emissions, many of which were toxic and non-biodegradable. The nature of waste shifted from predominantly organic to include a variety of industrial materials such as metals, chemicals, and synthetic compounds. These changes posed new challenges for waste management, as traditional methods like composting and simple land disposal proved inadequate for handling industrial waste.

Urbanization, a direct consequence of industrialization, further compounded the issue. As people flocked to cities in search of employment, urban centers experienced unprecedented growth. The population boom in cities led to increased residential waste, straining existing waste management systems. Streets overflowed with refuse, and sanitation became a pressing public health concern. The inadequacy of waste management infrastructure in rapidly growing cities underscored the need for more organized and efficient waste disposal methods.

The environmental impact of industrial waste was profound. Factories often discharged waste directly into rivers and streams, leading to significant water pollution. Air quality deteriorated as industrial emissions filled the atmosphere with pollutants. These environmental consequences highlighted the urgent need for regulatory frameworks to manage waste effectively and protect natural resources.

In response to these challenges, the late 19th and early 20th centuries witnessed the development of more structured waste management systems. Governments began to implement regulations aimed at controlling industrial emissions and waste disposal. This period saw the establishment of municipal waste collection services, which played a crucial role in managing urban waste. The introduction of sanitary landfills and waste incineration facilities marked significant advancements in waste management, offering more effective solutions for reducing waste volume and mitigating environmental impacts.

The rise of consumer culture in the 20th century, fueled by industrialization, further influenced waste generation. Mass production and the availability of affordable consumer goods led to increased consumption and, consequently, more waste. Packaging materials, particularly plastics, became ubiquitous, contributing to the growing waste stream. The disposable nature of many consumer products exacerbated the problem, as items were often discarded after a single use.

This era also saw the emergence of recycling as a response to the waste crisis. Recycling programs aimed to divert materials like paper, glass, and metals from landfills, promoting resource conservation and reducing environmental impact. The introduction of recycling represented a shift towards more sustainable waste management practices, reflecting a growing awareness of the need to balance industrial progress with environmental stewardship.

The environmental movements of the 1960s and 1970s brought increased attention to the consequences of industrial waste. Public awareness campaigns and landmark publications, such as Rachel Carson's "Silent Spring," underscored the ecological damage caused by industrial activities. This growing environmental consciousness led to the enactment of environmental regulations and the establishment of agencies tasked with monitoring and managing waste.

In recent decades, the influence of industrialization on waste generation has been further shaped by technological advancements and globalization. The development of new materials and production processes has introduced additional complexities to waste management. The global supply chain has increased the volume and diversity of waste, while electronic waste, or e-waste, has emerged as a significant challenge due to the rapid turnover of consumer electronics.

To address these challenges, contemporary waste management strategies emphasize the importance of reducing waste at its source. Industries are increasingly adopting sustainable practices, such as green manufacturing and circular economy principles, to minimize waste and maximize resource efficiency. These approaches focus on designing products for longevity, facilitating repair and recycling, and reducing the environmental footprint of production processes.

Collaboration among governments, industries, and communities is essential in managing the influence of industrialization on waste generation. International agreements, such as the Basel Convention, aim to regulate the movement and disposal of hazardous waste, promoting global cooperation in addressing waste challenges. Public-private partnerships and community engagement initiatives play vital roles in fostering sustainable waste management practices and encouraging responsible consumption.

The legacy of industrialization is a complex tapestry of progress and challenges. While it has fueled economic growth and technological innovation, it has also significantly impacted waste generation and environmental health. The ongoing task is to balance industrial development with sustainable waste management, ensuring that the benefits of progress do not come at the expense of the planet. By learning from the past and embracing innovative solutions, societies can work towards a future where waste is managed responsibly, preserving the environment for generations to come.

Key Challenges Facing the Waste Management Industry

The waste management industry, tasked with the critical role of managing society's refuse, faces an array of challenges that are as complex as they are pressing. These challenges stem from a variety of factors, including technological limitations, regulatory constraints, economic pressures, and evolving societal expectations. Addressing these issues requires a multifaceted approach that encompasses innovation, collaboration, and a commitment to sustainable practices.

One of the most significant challenges is the sheer volume of waste generated globally. As populations grow and consumer habits evolve, the amount of waste produced continues to rise at an alarming rate. Urban areas, in particular, are grappling with the demands of managing increasing waste volumes, often with limited space for disposal. This trend is further exacerbated by the proliferation of single-use products and packaging, which contribute significantly to the waste stream. The industry must find ways to efficiently manage and reduce waste volumes while ensuring that disposal methods are both environmentally sound and economically viable.

The composition of waste is also changing, presenting additional hurdles for waste management professionals. The rise of electronic waste, or e-waste, is a prime example. E-waste contains valuable materials, such as precious metals, as well as hazardous substances that pose environmental and health risks if not properly handled. The rapid turnover of electronic devices, driven by technological advancements and consumer demand, has led to an influx of e-waste that traditional waste management systems are ill-equipped to handle. Developing effective strategies for e-waste recycling and disposal is essential to mitigating its impact.

Regulatory challenges further complicate waste management efforts. The industry operates within a complex web of local, national, and international regulations that govern waste collection, treatment, and disposal. These regulations are essential for ensuring public health and environmental protection, but they can also impose significant compliance costs and administrative burdens on waste management companies. Navigating this regulatory landscape requires a deep understanding of legal requirements and the ability to adapt to changing policies.

Economic pressures are another formidable challenge facing the waste management industry. The costs associated with waste collection, transportation, treatment, and disposal can be substantial, particularly for municipalities with limited budgets. Moreover, the market for recycled materials is highly volatile, influenced by global economic conditions and fluctuations in commodity prices. This volatility can impact the financial viability of recycling programs, making it difficult for waste management entities to invest in long-term solutions. Balancing economic sustainability with environmental responsibility is a delicate task that requires strategic planning and innovative business models.

Public perception and behavior play a crucial role in shaping waste management practices. Encouraging individuals and businesses to reduce, reuse, and recycle is fundamental to effective waste management, yet changing entrenched behaviors remains a significant challenge. Public education campaigns and incentives are important tools for fostering a culture of sustainability, but they must be carefully designed to engage diverse audiences and address barriers to participation.

The infrastructure required to support modern waste management practices is another area of concern. Many existing facilities are outdated and unable to accommodate contemporary waste streams or advanced treatment technologies. Investing in infrastructure upgrades and the development of new facilities is critical to improving efficiency and expanding capacity. However, securing funding for these projects can be difficult, particularly in regions with competing public spending priorities.

Innovative technologies offer promising solutions to many of the challenges facing the waste management industry, yet their adoption is not without obstacles. Advanced sorting and processing technologies, for example, can enhance resource recovery and reduce landfill reliance. However, integrating these technologies into existing systems requires significant capital investment, technical expertise, and workforce training. Additionally, the implementation of new technologies must be carefully managed to ensure that they complement rather than disrupt established operations.

Climate change presents a broader, overarching challenge for the waste management industry. Waste management activities, particularly landfill operations, contribute to greenhouse gas emissions, which exacerbate climate change. Mitigating these emissions is a critical goal, requiring the adoption of practices that minimize environmental impact. This includes enhancing landfill gas capture and utilization, promoting composting and organic waste diversion, and supporting the development of waste-to-energy technologies that offer renewable energy solutions.

Collaboration and partnership are essential strategies for overcoming the multifaceted challenges faced by the waste management industry. Public-private partnerships can leverage the strengths of both sectors to develop innovative solutions, share knowledge, and pool resources. Cross-industry collaboration can also facilitate the exchange of best practices and drive progress toward common sustainability goals.

Lastly, global waste management challenges demand international cooperation. The transboundary nature of waste, especially hazardous waste, necessitates coordinated efforts to prevent illegal dumping and ensure safe disposal. International agreements and frameworks provide mechanisms for addressing these issues, promoting accountability, and fostering global solidarity in tackling waste challenges.

The waste management industry stands at a crossroads, confronted with challenges that are as diverse as they are daunting. Yet, within these challenges lie opportunities for transformation and progress. By embracing innovation, fostering collaboration, and committing to sustainable practices, the industry can navigate this complex landscape and contribute to a healthier, more sustainable planet. This journey requires a concerted effort from all stakeholders, from policymakers and industry leaders to communities and individuals, each playing a vital role in shaping the future of waste management.

Chapter 2: Emerging Technologies in Waste Management

The Role of Artificial Intelligence and Machine Learning

The integration of technology into waste management has ushered in a new era of efficiency and innovation, with artificial intelligence (AI) and machine learning (ML) at the forefront of this transformation. These technologies offer unprecedented opportunities to optimize waste management processes, enhance resource recovery, and reduce environmental impact, presenting a paradigm shift in how waste is perceived and managed.

AI and ML have the potential to revolutionize waste sorting and processing, two critical components of modern waste management. Traditional sorting methods often rely on manual labor, which can be time-consuming and prone to human error. AI-powered systems, however, can automate and refine these processes. Using advanced sensors and image recognition technologies, AI can accurately identify and categorize materials, ensuring that recyclables are efficiently separated from waste streams. This not only increases the purity and value of recyclables but also reduces contamination, a significant challenge in recycling operations.

Machine learning algorithms play a crucial role in enhancing the accuracy and adaptability of sorting technologies. By continuously analyzing data from sorting processes, ML can refine its algorithms, improving sorting precision over time. This adaptability is particularly valuable in managing complex waste streams that contain a wide variety of materials, from plastics and metals to organic waste.

AI's capabilities extend to waste collection and logistics, where it can optimize routes and schedules for waste collection vehicles. By analyzing traffic patterns, waste generation data, and environmental factors, AI can develop dynamic collection schedules that reduce fuel consumption, lower operational costs, and minimize the carbon footprint of waste collection activities. This optimization leads to more efficient use of resources and improved service delivery, benefiting both waste management companies and the communities they serve.

Predictive analytics, a key component of AI technology, offers significant benefits for waste management planning and decision-making. By analyzing historical data and identifying trends, AI can forecast future waste generation levels, enabling waste management authorities to plan infrastructure and resource allocation more effectively. This foresight is essential for accommodating population growth, urban development, and changes in consumption patterns that impact waste generation.

AI and ML also offer innovative solutions for landfill management. Intelligent monitoring systems equipped with AI can track landfill conditions in real-time, assessing factors such as temperature, gas emissions, and leachate levels. This continuous monitoring enables early detection of potential issues, such as methane leaks or groundwater contamination, allowing for timely interventions that mitigate environmental risks. Moreover, AI-driven models can predict the lifespan of landfills, informing strategic decisions about landfill expansion or the development of alternative waste treatment facilities.

Resource recovery, a critical aspect of sustainable waste management, is another area where AI and ML can make significant contributions. Advanced AI algorithms can identify patterns and correlations within waste streams, uncovering opportunities for recovering valuable materials that might otherwise be overlooked. For example, AI can assist in the extraction of rare metals from electronic waste or the identification of high-quality plastics suitable for recycling, turning waste into a valuable resource and promoting the circular economy.

The application of AI and ML in composting and organic waste management is yet another promising frontier. AI systems can monitor and control composting conditions, such as temperature and humidity, optimizing the decomposition process and ensuring the production of high-quality compost. This precision reduces the time required for composting and enhances the efficiency of organic waste recycling, contributing to sustainable agriculture and soil health.

While the benefits of AI and ML in waste management are substantial, their implementation is not without challenges. The adoption of these technologies requires significant investment in infrastructure and skilled personnel, as well as robust data management systems to support AI's data-driven nature. Additionally, the integration of AI into existing waste management practices must be carefully managed to ensure compatibility and avoid disruptions.

Data security and privacy are critical considerations in the deployment of AI and ML technologies. As these systems rely on vast amounts of data to function effectively, safeguarding this information against unauthorized access and ensuring compliance with data protection regulations is paramount. Transparent data policies and robust cybersecurity measures are essential to maintaining public trust and protecting sensitive information.

Collaboration and knowledge sharing are vital to advancing the role of AI and ML in waste management. Partnerships between technology developers, waste management companies, and regulatory bodies can facilitate the development and deployment of AI-driven solutions, ensuring that they align with industry needs and regulatory standards. Cross-sector collaboration can also promote the exchange of best practices and lessons learned, accelerating progress and innovation.

The role of AI and ML in waste management represents a transformative opportunity to enhance the efficiency, sustainability, and effectiveness of waste management practices. By harnessing the power of these technologies, the industry can not only address existing challenges but also reimagine waste as a resource, contributing to a more sustainable and resilient future. As AI and ML continue to evolve, their potential to drive positive change in waste management will only grow, underscoring the importance of embracing innovation and collaboration in the pursuit of sustainable solutions.

Robotics in Waste Sorting and Processing

Robotics has emerged as a powerful force in transforming waste sorting and processing, offering innovative solutions to some of the industry's most persistent challenges. As waste volumes increase and the complexity of materials grows, the need for efficient, precise, and scalable sorting systems becomes ever more critical. Robotics, with its ability to automate and enhance these processes, is paving the way for a more sustainable future in waste management.

The introduction of robotics into waste sorting processes addresses several key issues that have traditionally plagued the industry. One of the most significant challenges is the labor-intensive nature of manual sorting. Sorting waste by hand is not only time-consuming but also exposes workers to hazardous conditions and health risks. Robotics offers a safer alternative, automating the sorting process and reducing the need for human intervention. This automation not only protects workers but also increases efficiency and accuracy, as robots can operate continuously without fatigue.

Robots equipped with advanced sensors and machine vision technology can accurately identify and sort a wide range of materials. These systems use cameras, infrared sensors, and other detection technologies to analyze the composition of waste items as they pass along conveyor belts. By recognizing specific shapes, colors, and textures, robots can effectively differentiate between various types of recyclables, such as plastics, metals, and paper. This precision ensures that materials are sorted with a high degree of accuracy, reducing contamination and improving the quality of recycled outputs.

The adaptability of robotic systems is another significant advantage. As waste streams evolve and new materials are introduced, robots can be programmed or trained to recognize and sort these items. This flexibility is particularly valuable in managing complex waste streams that contain a diverse array of materials. Furthermore, robotic systems can be integrated into existing waste management infrastructure, complementing traditional sorting methods and enhancing overall system performance.

Robotic sorting systems are not limited to traditional waste management facilities; they are also being deployed in innovative contexts such as smart bins and decentralized recycling stations. Smart bins equipped with robotic sorting capabilities can be placed in urban areas, allowing for on-site separation of recyclables. This decentralized approach reduces the need for extensive transportation of waste materials, lowering emissions and operational costs while promoting recycling at the source.

The integration of robotics into waste processing extends beyond sorting. Robots can also assist in tasks such as shredding, compacting, and transporting waste materials within facilities. These applications streamline operations, improve material handling, and contribute to more efficient processing workflows. Additionally, robots can be employed in hazardous environments, such as electronic waste recycling plants, where they safely dismantle and process devices containing toxic substances.

While the benefits of robotics in waste sorting and processing are substantial, their implementation requires careful consideration. The initial investment in robotic systems can be significant, encompassing the cost of equipment, installation, and training. However, the long-term savings and efficiency gains often outweigh these upfront costs. Waste management companies must evaluate their specific needs and operational contexts to determine the most appropriate robotic solutions.

Another consideration is the need for skilled personnel to operate and maintain robotic systems. As the industry increasingly relies on technology, there is a growing demand for workers with expertise in robotics, engineering, and data analysis. Investing in workforce development and training programs is essential to ensure that employees are equipped with the skills needed to manage and optimize robotic systems effectively.

Collaboration and innovation are key to advancing the role of robotics in waste management. Partnerships between waste management companies, technology developers, and research institutions can drive the development of cutting-edge robotic solutions tailored to industry needs. These collaborations can also facilitate the sharing of best practices and lessons learned, accelerating the adoption of robotics and enhancing their impact.

The environmental benefits of robotics in waste sorting and processing are significant. By improving the efficiency and accuracy of sorting processes, robots contribute to higher recycling rates and reduced landfill dependency. This, in turn, conserves natural resources and minimizes the environmental footprint of waste management activities. Additionally, the automation of waste processing tasks reduces energy consumption and emissions, supporting broader sustainability goals.

Public perception and acceptance of robotics in waste management are also important factors to consider. As with any technological advancement, there may be concerns about job displacement and the implications of automation. Engaging with communities and stakeholders to communicate the benefits of robotics and address these concerns is crucial. By highlighting the potential for job creation in technology and engineering sectors, as well as the improved safety and environmental outcomes, the industry can foster a positive perception of robotics in waste management.

The future of waste management lies in the continued integration of robotics and automation. As technology advances and waste streams become increasingly complex, the role of robotics will only grow in importance. By embracing these innovations, the industry can enhance its efficiency, sustainability, and resilience, ensuring that waste management systems are equipped to meet the demands of a rapidly changing world. Robotics, with its ability to transform waste sorting and processing, represents a vital component of a sustainable waste management strategy, offering new opportunities to turn challenges into solutions.

Advanced Material Recovery Facilities

Advanced Material Recovery Facilities (MRFs) represent a pivotal evolution in the waste management landscape, providing sophisticated solutions for sorting and processing recyclable materials. As urban areas continue to expand and consumer waste grows in complexity, MRFs have become essential in efficiently managing the diverse waste streams produced by modern societies. These facilities are not only pivotal in enhancing recycling rates but also in minimizing the environmental footprint of waste management practices.

The inception of MRFs can be traced back to the need for more efficient sorting mechanisms as recycling became a central component of waste management strategies. Traditional methods, relying heavily on manual sorting, were often inefficient and unable to cope with the increasing volume and complexity of waste. Advanced MRFs address these limitations through the integration of cutting-edge technologies that streamline operations and maximize the recovery of valuable materials.

A key feature of advanced MRFs is their ability to process mixed waste streams. Unlike older systems that required pre-sorted materials, modern facilities can handle commingled recyclables, thanks to sophisticated sorting technologies. This capability significantly enhances the convenience and efficiency of recycling programs, as it reduces the need for extensive pre-sorting by consumers and waste collection services.

Within these facilities, a combination of mechanical and automated sorting techniques is employed to separate materials with precision. Mechanical systems such as trommels, screens, and conveyors are used to sort materials by size and density. Meanwhile, automated technologies, including optical sorters, magnetic separators, and eddy current separators, provide the capability to identify and categorize materials based on their composition. Optical sorters, for instance, use near-infrared sensors and cameras to detect different types of plastics, paper, and other recyclables, ensuring accurate separation.

The implementation of robotics and machine learning algorithms further enhances sorting efficiency and accuracy. Robotic arms equipped with advanced sensors and AI-driven systems can identify and pick specific items from conveyor belts, allowing for rapid and precise sorting of materials that might otherwise be missed by traditional methods. These robots can be programmed to adapt to changing waste streams, learning to recognize new materials as they are introduced into the recycling ecosystem.

One of the primary advantages of advanced MRFs is their ability to increase the purity and quality of recovered materials. By employing state-of-the-art sorting technologies, these facilities can reduce contamination levels in recyclable outputs, making them more valuable and marketable. This improvement in quality is crucial for maintaining the economic viability of recycling programs, as it ensures that recovered materials meet the stringent standards required by manufacturers and end-users.

Energy efficiency and sustainability are also central to the design and operation of advanced MRFs. Many facilities incorporate energy-saving technologies, such as high-efficiency motors and lighting systems, to minimize their environmental impact. Additionally, some MRFs are equipped with renewable energy sources, such as solar panels or wind turbines, further reducing their carbon footprint and aligning with broader sustainability goals.

The role of data analytics in optimizing MRF operations cannot be overstated. Advanced MRFs leverage data-driven insights to monitor and improve their performance continuously. By analyzing operational data, facility managers can identify bottlenecks, assess equipment efficiency, and make informed decisions about process improvements. This data-centric approach enhances the overall efficiency and effectiveness of waste recovery processes, ensuring that facilities remain responsive to changing waste management needs.

Community engagement and education are integral components of successful MRF operations. By fostering awareness and understanding of the recycling process, MRFs can encourage greater participation in recycling programs and reduce contamination in collected materials. Educational initiatives, such as facility tours and outreach programs, help demystify the recycling process for the public, highlighting the critical role that individuals play in supporting sustainable waste management practices.

Despite the many benefits offered by advanced MRFs, their implementation is not without challenges. The initial capital investment required for building and equipping these facilities can be substantial, posing financial barriers for some municipalities and waste management companies. Additionally, the rapid pace of technological advancement necessitates ongoing investment in equipment upgrades and workforce training to ensure that facilities remain at the forefront of industry standards.

The integration of advanced MRFs into existing waste management systems also requires careful planning and coordination. Collaboration between local governments, waste management companies, and technology providers is essential to ensure that facilities are designed and operated in a way that meets the specific needs and priorities of the communities they serve. This collaborative approach can also facilitate the sharing of best practices and innovations, fostering continuous improvement across the industry.

Policy and regulatory frameworks play a crucial role in supporting the development and success of advanced MRFs. Governments can incentivize the establishment and operation of these facilities through grants, tax breaks, and other financial mechanisms. Additionally, policies that promote extended producer responsibility and circular economy principles can drive demand for high-quality recycled materials, ensuring that advanced MRFs remain economically viable.

The future of waste management is inextricably linked to the continued evolution of advanced MRFs. As waste streams become increasingly diverse and complex, these facilities will be instrumental in maximizing resource recovery and minimizing environmental impact. By embracing innovation and fostering collaboration, the waste management industry can harness the full potential of advanced MRFs, turning waste into a valuable resource and paving the way for a more sustainable future. These facilities represent not only a technological advancement but a fundamental shift in how societies perceive and manage waste, underscoring the importance of innovation and sustainability in addressing the challenges of modern waste management.

Innovations in Biodegradable and Compostable Materials

Biodegradable and compostable materials have emerged as pivotal innovations in the quest for sustainable waste management. As environmental concerns intensify and the detrimental impact of traditional plastics becomes increasingly evident, the development and use of these materials offer a promising path forward. They present a viable alternative to conventional plastics, reducing landfill waste and mitigating pollution while supporting a circular economy.

The distinction between biodegradable and compostable materials is essential for understanding their role and potential impact. Biodegradable materials are those that can be broken down by natural processes into water, carbon dioxide, and biomass over time. Compostable materials, on the other hand, are a subset of biodegradable materials that decompose under specific conditions, typically in an industrial composting facility, into nutrient-rich compost without leaving toxic residues.

The drive to innovate in this field stems from the pressing need to address the global plastic waste crisis. Plastics, derived from fossil fuels, are renowned for their durability and resistance to degradation, which translates into a persistent environmental problem. Traditional plastics can take hundreds of years to break down, leading to significant accumulation in landfills and natural ecosystems, where they pose a threat to wildlife and human health.

Biodegradable and compostable materials offer a solution to this issue by providing products that can return to the earth safely. These materials are often derived from renewable resources such as corn starch, sugarcane, and cellulose, which are converted into polymers that mimic the properties of traditional plastics. This transformation is achieved through advanced chemical processes and innovations in material science, allowing for the creation of products that can perform similarly to conventional plastics in terms of strength, flexibility, and durability.

The potential applications for biodegradable and compostable materials are vast and diverse. In the packaging industry, these materials are being used to create everything from shopping bags and food wrappers to disposable cutlery and plates. This shift is particularly evident in sectors such as food service and retail, where single-use plastics have traditionally dominated. By replacing these items with biodegradable alternatives, businesses can significantly reduce their environmental footprint and contribute to a more sustainable future.

In agriculture, biodegradable mulches and plant pots offer an eco-friendly alternative to traditional plastic products. These materials can be used to cover soil, suppress weeds, and retain moisture, eventually breaking down and enriching the soil without the need for removal or disposal. This not only reduces waste but also enhances soil health and crop yields, supporting more sustainable agricultural practices.

The development of compostable materials has also revolutionized the waste management landscape by providing a more sustainable option for organic waste disposal. Compostable products can be collected alongside food scraps and other organic waste, processed in industrial composting facilities, and transformed into nutrient-rich compost. This compost can then be used to improve soil quality and support plant growth, closing the loop in a circular system that minimizes waste and maximizes resource recovery.

Despite their promise, the widespread adoption of biodegradable and compostable materials faces several challenges. One of the primary obstacles is the need for appropriate infrastructure to support their decomposition. While these materials can break down in industrial composting facilities, they often require specific conditions, such as high temperatures and humidity, to do so efficiently. Without the necessary infrastructure, these materials may end up in landfills, where they decompose at a much slower rate, negating their environmental benefits.

Another challenge is consumer confusion surrounding the terms "biodegradable" and "compostable." Many people mistakenly believe that these materials can break down in any environment, including home compost bins or natural settings, when in reality, they often require industrial conditions. Clear labeling and public education are essential to ensure that consumers understand how to properly dispose of these materials and maximize their environmental benefits.

Cost is another consideration that can impact the adoption of biodegradable and compostable materials. While prices have decreased as production processes have become more efficient, these materials can still be more expensive than traditional plastics. This cost differential can be a barrier for businesses and consumers, particularly in price-sensitive markets. However, as demand grows and technological advancements continue, economies of scale are expected to further reduce costs, making these materials more accessible and competitive.

Innovation in biodegradable and compostable materials is ongoing, with researchers exploring new sources and processes to enhance their performance and reduce costs. Advances in biotechnology, for example, are enabling the development of materials from waste products, such as agricultural residues and food waste, which can be transformed into valuable bioplastics. These efforts not only contribute to waste reduction but also create new economic opportunities and support sustainable development.

Collaboration across industries and sectors is crucial to advancing the use and effectiveness of biodegradable and compostable materials. Partnerships between manufacturers, waste management companies, governments, and research institutions can drive innovation, facilitate knowledge sharing, and support the development of necessary infrastructure. By working together, stakeholders can overcome existing challenges and unlock the full potential of these materials to drive environmental and economic benefits.

The role of policy and regulation is also vital in promoting the adoption of biodegradable and compostable materials. Governments can implement policies that incentivize the use of sustainable materials, such as tax breaks, subsidies, or mandates for certain products. Additionally, regulations that standardize labeling and certification can help ensure that products meet environmental performance criteria and provide clear guidance for consumers.

The future of waste management and environmental sustainability is closely intertwined with the development and adoption of biodegradable and compostable materials. By embracing these innovations and addressing the challenges associated with their use, societies can transition towards more sustainable consumption and production patterns. This shift not only reduces the environmental impact of waste but also fosters a circular economy where resources are used efficiently and responsibly, ensuring a healthier planet for future generations.

The Impact of IoT on Waste Management Efficiency

The Internet of Things (IoT) is rapidly transforming industries worldwide, and its impact on waste management is particularly profound. This interconnected network of devices and systems offers the potential to revolutionize waste management practices, enhancing efficiency, reducing costs, and minimizing environmental impact. By leveraging IoT technologies, waste management systems can become more data-driven, adaptive, and responsive to the dynamic challenges of urban environments.

At the core of IoT's influence on waste management is the ability to collect and analyze real-time data from a multitude of sources. Smart sensors, embedded in waste bins, vehicles, and facilities, continuously monitor and transmit data regarding waste levels, temperature, humidity, and other pertinent factors. This wealth of information provides a comprehensive overview of waste generation patterns, enabling waste management authorities to make informed decisions and optimize their operations.

One of the most significant advantages of IoT in waste management is the optimization of waste collection processes. Traditionally, waste collection routes are predetermined and operate on fixed schedules, often leading to inefficiencies such as emptying bins that are only partially full or overlooking those that are overflowing. IoT-enabled smart bins equipped with fill-level sensors can communicate their status to a centralized system, which then analyzes the data to dynamically adjust collection routes and schedules. This results in more efficient allocation of resources, reduced fuel consumption, and lower greenhouse gas emissions.

In addition to optimizing collection routes, IoT technology facilitates predictive maintenance of waste management equipment. Sensors integrated into waste collection vehicles and processing machinery can monitor the condition of components and alert operators to potential issues before they lead to costly breakdowns. This proactive approach to maintenance ensures that equipment remains in optimal working condition, reducing downtime and extending the lifespan of assets.

IoT's role in waste management extends beyond collection and maintenance; it also enhances the efficiency of waste processing and treatment facilities. By monitoring parameters such as temperature, pressure, and chemical composition, IoT devices can provide real-time insights into the performance of waste treatment processes. This data allows operators to fine-tune operations, maximize resource recovery, and minimize emissions and energy consumption.

The integration of IoT with waste management infrastructure also supports the development of smart waste management systems that can adapt to the unique needs of different communities. For instance, urban areas with high population densities may generate large volumes of waste that require frequent collection and processing, while rural areas may have different waste management challenges. IoT technology enables waste management systems to tailor their operations to the specific demands of each community, ensuring that resources are used efficiently and effectively.

IoT also plays a crucial role in promoting transparency and accountability within waste management systems. By providing stakeholders with access to real-time data on waste generation, collection, and processing, IoT technology fosters greater awareness and understanding of waste management practices. This transparency can lead to increased public trust and engagement, encouraging communities to participate in recycling and waste reduction initiatives.

The deployment of IoT in waste management, however, is not without its challenges. One of the primary concerns is data security and privacy. As IoT devices collect and transmit vast amounts of data, ensuring the security of this information is paramount. Robust cybersecurity measures must be implemented to protect sensitive data from unauthorized access and breaches. Additionally, clear data governance policies are needed to address privacy concerns and ensure compliance with relevant regulations.

Another challenge is the initial investment required to implement IoT technologies in waste management systems. The cost of smart sensors, communication networks, and data analytics platforms can be significant, posing financial barriers for some municipalities and waste management companies. However, the long-term benefits of increased efficiency and reduced operational costs often justify the initial investment, and various financing options and partnerships can help mitigate these challenges.

Interoperability is another consideration when integrating IoT with existing waste management infrastructure. Ensuring that IoT devices and systems can communicate seamlessly with one another and with legacy equipment is crucial for maximizing the benefits of these technologies. Industry standards and protocols play a vital role in facilitating interoperability and enabling the widespread adoption of IoT solutions.

The impact of IoT on waste management is further enhanced by its potential to support data-driven policy and decision-making. By providing comprehensive insights into waste generation and management practices, IoT technology can inform the development of policies and regulations that promote sustainability and resource efficiency. Data analytics can also identify trends and patterns that may indicate areas for improvement or highlight successful initiatives that can be replicated elsewhere.

Collaboration and innovation are key to unlocking the full potential of IoT in waste management. Partnerships between technology providers, waste management companies, and government agencies can drive the development of innovative solutions and facilitate the sharing of best practices and lessons learned. By working together, stakeholders can overcome challenges and accelerate the adoption of IoT technologies, enhancing the efficiency and sustainability of waste management systems.

The future of waste management is increasingly intertwined with the advancement of IoT technologies. As these technologies continue to evolve and mature, their impact on waste management efficiency will only grow, offering new opportunities to address the challenges of urbanization, resource scarcity, and environmental degradation. By embracing the potential of IoT, waste management systems can become more responsive, adaptive, and sustainable, paving the way for a cleaner and more resilient future. Through innovation and collaboration, IoT can transform waste management from a reactive process into a proactive strategy, ensuring that resources are used wisely and waste is managed responsibly for generations to come.

Chapter 3: Waste-to-Energy Solutions

Overview of Waste Incineration and Gasification

Waste incineration and gasification are two pivotal technologies in the realm of waste management, offering distinct approaches to handling waste materials. As global urbanization accelerates and waste production surges, the pressure to find effective waste treatment methods grows correspondingly. Both incineration and gasification serve as solutions to reduce the volume of waste destined for landfills while simultaneously generating energy. However, they differ significantly in their processes, efficiencies, and environmental impacts.

Incineration is a well-established waste treatment process that involves the combustion of organic substances contained in waste materials. This method reduces waste volume by approximately 70 to 90 percent, making it an attractive option for urban areas where land is scarce and landfill space is limited. The incineration process takes place in high-temperature furnaces where waste is burned, converting it into ash, flue gas, and heat. This heat can be harnessed to generate energy, often in the form of electricity or steam, thus contributing to energy recovery efforts.

A primary advantage of waste incineration is its ability to handle a wide variety of waste types, including municipal solid waste, hazardous waste, and medical waste. This versatility makes it a critical component of integrated waste management systems, especially in regions with diverse waste streams. Additionally, incineration offers a significant reduction in waste mass and volume, decreasing the burden on landfills and extending their operational lifespans.

Despite these benefits, incineration has faced criticism due to concerns about its environmental impact. The combustion process releases emissions, including carbon dioxide, particulate matter, and potentially harmful pollutants such as dioxins and furans. To address these concerns, modern waste incineration facilities are equipped with advanced air pollution control technologies, such as electrostatic precipitators, fabric filters, and scrubbers, to capture and neutralize hazardous emissions. Continuous monitoring and stringent regulatory standards further ensure that emissions remain within safe limits.

Gasification, on the other hand, is an emerging waste treatment technology that offers a cleaner alternative to traditional incineration. This process involves the conversion of carbonaceous materials into syngas, a mixture of hydrogen, carbon monoxide, and carbon dioxide, by reacting the material at high temperatures with a controlled amount of oxygen. Unlike incineration, gasification is a thermochemical process that does not involve combustion. This distinction results in lower emissions of pollutants and a potentially higher energy recovery efficiency.

The syngas produced from gasification can be used as a fuel for generating electricity or as a feedstock for producing chemicals and fuels. This flexibility makes gasification an attractive option for waste-to-energy applications, as it can be integrated into existing energy infrastructure and contribute to the generation of renewable energy. Furthermore, gasification allows for the recovery of valuable metals and minerals from waste, reducing the need for raw material extraction and supporting circular economy principles.

One of the challenges associated with gasification is the need for consistent and homogeneous feedstock to ensure efficient and stable operation. This requirement can limit the types of waste that can be effectively processed through gasification, necessitating careful sorting and preprocessing of materials. Additionally, the initial capital investment and operational costs of gasification facilities can be higher than those of traditional incineration plants, posing financial barriers for widespread adoption.

The potential environmental benefits of gasification over incineration have spurred interest and investment in its development and deployment. However, the technology is still evolving, and further research and innovation are needed to address technical challenges and optimize its performance. Pilot projects and demonstration plants play a crucial role in advancing gasification technology, providing valuable insights and data that can inform future commercial-scale implementations.

While both incineration and gasification offer viable solutions for waste management, their roles and impacts must be carefully considered within the broader context of sustainable waste management strategies. Each technology has its strengths and limitations, and their suitability depends on factors such as waste composition, local infrastructure, regulatory frameworks, and community preferences.

In regions where waste composition is heterogeneous and landfill space is scarce, incineration may be the more practical choice due to its ability to handle diverse waste streams and reduce waste volume significantly. Conversely, in areas with access to consistent and high-quality feedstock, gasification may be preferred for its potential to achieve higher energy recovery efficiencies and lower emissions.

The integration of incineration and gasification into waste management systems requires careful planning and collaboration among stakeholders, including government agencies, waste management companies, technology providers, and local communities. Public engagement and education are essential to address concerns and misconceptions about waste-to-energy technologies and to build trust and support for their implementation.

Policy and regulatory frameworks play a critical role in shaping the development and deployment of incineration and gasification technologies. Governments can incentivize the adoption of cleaner and more efficient waste treatment methods through subsidies, grants, and tax breaks. Additionally, setting stringent emission standards and promoting research and development can drive innovation and continuous improvement in waste management practices.

The future of waste treatment lies in the continued advancement and integration of technologies like incineration and gasification, alongside other waste management strategies such as recycling, composting, and waste reduction. By embracing a holistic and flexible approach, societies can address the growing challenges of waste management while minimizing environmental impact and maximizing resource recovery. These technologies represent vital components of a sustainable waste management system, offering pathways to transform waste from a burden into a valuable resource and contributing to a more sustainable and resilient future for all.

Anaerobic Digestion and Biogas Production

Anaerobic digestion is a biological process that breaks down organic matter in the absence of oxygen, resulting in the production of biogas and digestate. This process occurs naturally in environments such as wetlands and animal digestive systems but can be harnessed and optimized in controlled conditions to manage waste and generate renewable energy. The potential of anaerobic digestion as a sustainable waste management solution is significant, particularly in the context of organic waste, which constitutes a substantial portion of municipal solid waste worldwide.

The process of anaerobic digestion involves a series of complex biochemical reactions carried out by different groups of microorganisms. These microorganisms work synergistically to convert complex organic materials, such as carbohydrates, proteins, and fats, into simpler compounds. The process can be divided into four main stages: hydrolysis, acidogenesis, acetogenesis, and methanogenesis. Each stage is crucial for the successful breakdown of organic matter and the efficient production of biogas.

In the hydrolysis stage, complex organic polymers are broken down into simpler monomers by hydrolytic microorganisms. This step is often the rate-limiting stage of anaerobic digestion, as the breakdown of large molecules into smaller ones can be slow. Following hydrolysis, the acidogenesis stage sees the conversion of monomers into volatile fatty acids, alcohols, hydrogen, and carbon dioxide by acidogenic bacteria. Acetogenesis then takes over, where acetogenic bacteria convert these intermediate products into acetic acid, hydrogen, and carbon dioxide. Finally, methanogenesis is carried out by methanogenic archaea, which convert the acetic acid, hydrogen, and carbon dioxide into methane and water, resulting in the production of biogas.

Biogas, a mixture primarily composed of methane and carbon dioxide, is a valuable renewable energy source. When captured and utilized, biogas can be used to generate electricity and heat or can be upgraded to biomethane, a substitute for natural gas. This versatility makes biogas an attractive component of renewable energy portfolios, contributing to energy security and the reduction of greenhouse gas emissions.

The digestate, the solid and liquid residue remaining after anaerobic digestion, is rich in nutrients and can be used as a bio-fertilizer in agriculture. This application not only recycles nutrients back into the soil but also reduces the need for chemical fertilizers, promoting sustainable agricultural practices and enhancing soil health.

Anaerobic digestion is particularly well-suited for treating various types of organic waste, including food waste, agricultural residues, wastewater sludge, and animal manure. By diverting organic waste from landfills, anaerobic digestion reduces landfill emissions, mitigates odors, and prevents the leaching of harmful substances into the environment. Additionally, the process contributes to the circular economy by transforming waste into valuable resources such as energy and bio-fertilizer.

Despite its advantages, the implementation of anaerobic digestion systems poses several challenges. The efficiency of the process is influenced by factors such as temperature, pH, feedstock composition, and retention time. Mesophilic and thermophilic conditions are commonly used to optimize the digestion process. Mesophilic digestion occurs at moderate temperatures (around 35-40°C), while thermophilic digestion takes place at higher temperatures (50-60°C) and typically results in faster digestion rates and higher pathogen reduction. However, thermophilic systems require more energy input and careful temperature control.

Feedstock composition is another critical factor affecting the performance of anaerobic digestion systems. The presence of inhibitory substances, such as high concentrations of ammonia or sulfates, can disrupt microbial activity and reduce biogas yields. Therefore, careful selection and pretreatment of feedstock are essential to ensure optimal digestion conditions. Co-digestion, the simultaneous digestion of multiple feedstocks, can enhance process stability and biogas production by balancing nutrient levels and providing a more homogeneous substrate.

Economic considerations also play a significant role in the adoption of anaerobic digestion technology. The initial capital investment for building and commissioning anaerobic digestion plants can be substantial, particularly for large-scale facilities. However, the long-term benefits, including energy savings, waste disposal cost reductions, and revenue from biogas and digestate sales, often offset the initial investment. Financial incentives, such as feed-in tariffs, renewable energy credits, and government grants, can further enhance the economic viability of anaerobic digestion projects.

The success of anaerobic digestion systems relies heavily on the integration of technology, policy, and community engagement. Technological advancements continue to improve the efficiency and cost-effectiveness of anaerobic digestion processes. Innovations such as automated monitoring systems, advanced microbial consortia, and enhanced reactor designs contribute to the optimization of biogas production and process stability.

Policy frameworks play a crucial role in promoting the adoption of anaerobic digestion technology. Governments can support the deployment of anaerobic digestion systems through regulatory measures, financial incentives, and the establishment of favorable market conditions for biogas and digestate products. Policies that encourage the diversion of organic waste from landfills and promote renewable energy generation can drive the expansion of anaerobic digestion infrastructure.

Community engagement and education are also vital for the successful implementation of anaerobic digestion projects. Public awareness of the environmental and economic benefits of anaerobic digestion can foster greater acceptance and participation in waste segregation and collection programs. Collaboration between stakeholders, including waste generators, technology providers, policymakers, and local communities, is essential to ensure that anaerobic digestion systems are designed and operated to meet local needs and priorities.

The future of anaerobic digestion and biogas production holds great promise in the transition towards sustainable waste management and renewable energy systems. As technology continues to evolve and policy frameworks support the integration of anaerobic digestion into waste management strategies, the potential for this technology to contribute to environmental protection, resource recovery, and energy generation will only increase. By embracing anaerobic digestion, societies can transform organic waste from a burden into a valuable resource, promoting a more sustainable and resilient future for all.

Emerging Trends in Pyrolysis Technology

Pyrolysis technology is making significant strides as an innovative solution for waste management and energy production. This process involves the thermal decomposition of organic materials in the absence of oxygen, resulting in the production of solid, liquid, and gaseous products. As the world grapples with growing waste challenges and the imperative for sustainable energy, pyrolysis offers a promising avenue to convert waste into valuable resources while reducing environmental impact.

One of the most compelling aspects of pyrolysis technology is its versatility in handling a wide range of feedstocks. From plastic waste and biomass to used tires and agricultural residues, pyrolysis can process diverse materials, transforming them into products such as biochar, pyrolysis oil, and syngas. This flexibility makes it an attractive option for addressing the varied waste streams generated in different sectors and regions.

Biochar, one of the solid products of pyrolysis, has garnered attention for its potential applications in agriculture and environmental management. Rich in carbon, biochar can be used as a soil amendment to enhance soil fertility, improve water retention, and sequester carbon. Its porous structure provides a habitat for beneficial soil microorganisms, promoting healthier plant growth. Additionally, biochar's ability to adsorb pollutants makes it useful for soil remediation and water filtration applications, contributing to environmental sustainability.

Pyrolysis oil, or bio-oil, is a liquid product that can be refined and upgraded to produce biofuels and chemicals. This aspect of pyrolysis aligns with the global shift towards renewable energy sources and the reduction of reliance on fossil fuels. By converting waste into bio-oil, pyrolysis not only addresses waste management issues but also contributes to the diversification of energy sources and the reduction of greenhouse gas emissions.

Syngas, the gaseous product of pyrolysis, consists mainly of hydrogen, carbon monoxide, and methane. It can be used as a fuel for power generation or as a feedstock for the production of chemicals and synthetic fuels. The utilization of syngas in energy systems supports the transition towards cleaner and more sustainable energy solutions.

Emerging trends in pyrolysis technology are focused on enhancing efficiency, scalability, and environmental performance. One such trend is the development of advanced reactor designs. Traditional pyrolysis reactors, such as fixed-bed and fluidized-bed reactors, are being improved to increase heat transfer efficiency and product yield. Innovations like microwave-assisted pyrolysis and plasma pyrolysis are gaining attention for their ability to achieve rapid heating and high energy efficiency, resulting in faster processing times and reduced energy consumption.

Microwave-assisted pyrolysis utilizes microwave radiation to heat materials from the inside out, ensuring uniform temperature distribution and enhancing the quality of the pyrolysis products. This method is particularly suitable for processing high-moisture feedstocks, such as food waste and sewage sludge, which can be challenging to handle with conventional heating techniques. Plasma pyrolysis, on the other hand, employs plasma arcs to generate extremely high temperatures, enabling the breakdown of complex and recalcitrant materials like plastics and tires into simpler compounds with minimal residue.

Another emerging trend is the integration of pyrolysis with other waste management and energy systems. For instance, coupling pyrolysis with anaerobic digestion can optimize the utilization of organic waste by converting the solid fraction into biochar and the liquid fraction into biogas. This integrated approach maximizes resource recovery and enhances the overall sustainability of waste management systems.

The development of hybrid pyrolysis systems, which combine pyrolysis with gasification or combustion, is also gaining traction. These systems aim to improve energy efficiency and product quality by leveraging the strengths of each process. For example, the gas produced during pyrolysis can be used to fuel the gasification or combustion process, reducing the need for external energy inputs and minimizing emissions.

The application of machine learning and data analytics in pyrolysis technology is another trend that is driving advancements in process optimization and control. By analyzing large datasets generated during pyrolysis operations, machine learning algorithms can identify patterns and correlations that inform process improvements, such as optimizing temperature profiles, residence times, and feedstock blends. This data-driven approach enhances the efficiency and reliability of pyrolysis systems, enabling operators to achieve consistent and high-quality outputs.

Despite the exciting advancements in pyrolysis technology, several challenges remain. The economic viability of pyrolysis projects is a critical consideration, as the costs associated with plant construction, operation, and maintenance can be substantial. However, the value derived from the products of pyrolysis, coupled with potential revenue from carbon credits and waste disposal fees, can offset these costs. Policymakers and industry stakeholders can play a role in supporting the adoption of pyrolysis technology by providing financial incentives, fostering research and development, and establishing clear regulatory frameworks.

Another challenge is the need for standardized product specifications and quality control measures. The variability in feedstock composition and process conditions can result in differences in the quality of pyrolysis products, affecting their marketability and end-use applications. Developing industry standards and certification schemes can enhance the acceptance and commercialization of pyrolysis products, facilitating their integration into existing markets and supply chains.

Public perception and acceptance of pyrolysis technology are also essential for its widespread adoption. Educating communities about the environmental and economic benefits of pyrolysis can build trust and support for the establishment of pyrolysis facilities. Engaging with stakeholders, including local residents, environmental organizations, and industry representatives, can foster collaboration and address potential concerns related to emissions, odors, and other environmental impacts.

The future of pyrolysis technology is promising, with ongoing research and innovation poised to unlock its full potential. By addressing existing challenges and capitalizing on emerging trends, pyrolysis can play a pivotal role in transforming waste management practices and contributing to a more sustainable and circular economy. As societies continue to seek solutions for managing waste and reducing environmental impact, pyrolysis technology offers a pathway to convert waste into valuable resources, supporting the transition towards a cleaner and more resilient future. Through continued collaboration, investment, and innovation, the potential of pyrolysis can be realized to benefit both people and the planet.

The Economics of Waste-to-Energy Conversion

Waste-to-energy (WtE) conversion presents a compelling solution for managing waste sustainably while generating energy. This innovative approach transforms waste materials into usable energy forms, such as electricity, heat, or fuel, thereby addressing two critical global challenges: waste management and energy demand. However, the economic viability of waste-to-energy conversion is a crucial factor that shapes its adoption and implementation across different regions and sectors.

The economics of waste-to-energy conversion are influenced by several key factors, including capital investment, operational costs, revenue streams, and market conditions. Understanding these factors is essential for evaluating the feasibility of WtE projects and making informed decisions about their development and deployment.

Capital investment represents one of the most significant financial considerations for waste-to-energy projects. Building and commissioning WtE facilities require substantial upfront expenditures, which can vary depending on the technology employed, the scale of the facility, and local infrastructure requirements. Incineration, gasification, and anaerobic digestion are among the primary technologies used in WtE processes, each with its own cost profile and technical specifications. The choice of technology impacts not only the initial investment but also the operational efficiency and environmental performance of the facility.

Operational costs encompass a wide range of expenses, including labor, maintenance, feedstock procurement, and energy consumption. Efficient management of these costs is vital to ensuring the long-term profitability of WtE facilities. For instance, optimizing feedstock procurement through strategic partnerships with waste generators can help secure a steady supply of materials and reduce costs associated with waste collection and transportation. Additionally, investing in energy-efficient technologies and practices can minimize energy consumption and enhance the overall economic performance of WtE operations.

Revenue generation is a critical component of the economic model for waste-to-energy conversion. WtE facilities generate revenue through the sale of energy products, such as electricity and heat, as well as by-products like biochar, syngas, and digestate. Furthermore, WtE projects can benefit from tipping fees charged for waste disposal, creating an additional income stream. The level of revenue generated depends on factors such as market demand, energy prices, and the quality of the products produced. In regions where energy prices are high or where there is strong demand for renewable energy, WtE facilities may achieve higher revenue and profitability.

Government policies and incentives play a pivotal role in shaping the economic landscape of waste-to-energy conversion. Supportive policies, such as feed-in tariffs, renewable energy credits, and tax incentives, can enhance the financial viability of WtE projects by providing stable income streams and reducing the cost burden. Additionally, regulatory frameworks that prioritize waste diversion from landfills and promote sustainable waste management practices can create favorable conditions for the development of WtE infrastructure.

The integration of waste-to-energy conversion into broader waste management and energy systems can also yield economic benefits. By reducing the volume of waste sent to landfills, WtE projects can extend landfill lifespans and decrease landfill-related costs, such as environmental monitoring and remediation. Furthermore, the generation of renewable energy through WtE contributes to energy diversification and security, potentially reducing reliance on imported fossil fuels and enhancing energy resilience.

While the economic benefits of waste-to-energy conversion are substantial, challenges remain that can impact the financial performance of WtE projects. Market volatility, such as fluctuations in energy prices and demand, can affect revenue stability and profitability. Additionally, the complexity of navigating regulatory environments and obtaining necessary permits can pose barriers to project development and implementation.

Public perception and acceptance of waste-to-energy projects are also critical to their success and economic sustainability. Engaging with communities and stakeholders to build awareness and understanding of the environmental and economic benefits of WtE can foster support and facilitate project approval. Transparent communication and collaboration with local residents, environmental organizations, and industry representatives can help address concerns related to emissions, odors, and other potential impacts.

Innovations in waste-to-energy technology and process optimization continue to drive economic improvements in the sector. Advances in reactor design, automation, and data analytics enhance efficiency and product quality, reducing operational costs and increasing revenue potential. Research and development efforts focused on diversifying feedstock, improving conversion efficiencies, and expanding end-use applications for WtE products can further strengthen the economic case for waste-to-energy conversion.

Partnerships and collaborations between public and private sectors are essential for advancing the economics of waste-to-energy projects. Public-private partnerships can leverage resources, expertise, and funding to support the development and operation of WtE facilities. These collaborations can also facilitate knowledge sharing and innovation, driving continuous improvement in waste management practices and technologies.

The future of waste-to-energy conversion is closely tied to the evolving economic, environmental, and social landscape. As societies seek sustainable solutions to address waste and energy challenges, the economic viability of WtE projects will play a critical role in their adoption and success. By understanding and addressing the economic factors that influence waste-to-energy conversion, stakeholders can unlock the potential of this technology to contribute to a more sustainable and resilient future.

Through strategic investment, policy support, technological innovation, and stakeholder engagement, the economics of waste-to-energy conversion can be optimized to maximize benefits for both people and the environment. As the global community continues to prioritize sustainability and resource efficiency, waste-to-energy conversion stands as a vital component of integrated waste management and renewable energy strategies. By harnessing the economic potential of waste-to-energy technologies, societies can transform waste from a challenge into an opportunity, driving progress towards a cleaner and more sustainable world.

Environmental Considerations and Challenges

Understanding the environmental considerations and challenges associated with waste-to-energy (WtE) technologies is crucial for their development and implementation. These technologies offer a dual benefit: they can help manage the ever-growing piles of waste while simultaneously contributing to energy production. However, balancing these benefits with potential environmental impacts requires careful analysis and planning. As societies strive for sustainability, the environmental implications of WtE systems must be thoroughly examined to ensure they align with broader ecological goals.

One of the primary environmental considerations of WtE technologies is air quality. The combustion processes used in technologies such as incineration can release pollutants into the atmosphere. These emissions may include carbon dioxide, nitrogen oxides, sulfur dioxide, and particulate matter, all of which can contribute to air pollution and have adverse effects on human health and the environment. Advanced air pollution control technologies are essential in mitigating these emissions. Techniques such as flue gas scrubbing, selective catalytic reduction, and electrostatic precipitators are commonly employed to capture and neutralize harmful pollutants before they are released into the atmosphere.

Another significant concern is the potential release of toxic substances, such as dioxins and heavy metals, during combustion processes. These substances have long-term environmental and health implications, necessitating stringent monitoring and regulation. Modern WtE facilities are equipped with state-of-the-art emission control systems and are subject to rigorous environmental standards to ensure that emissions remain within safe limits. Continuous emissions monitoring systems provide real-time data, enabling operators to maintain compliance and address any deviations promptly.

Water usage and contamination are also important environmental considerations in WtE systems. The cooling processes used in incineration and gasification can consume significant amounts of water, impacting local water resources, especially in arid regions. Additionally, the potential for leachate generation and contamination from waste processing residues must be managed to prevent soil and water pollution. Implementing closed-loop water systems and efficient wastewater treatment technologies can help minimize water consumption and mitigate contamination risks.

Land use and ecological impacts are other factors that must be considered when developing WtE facilities. The construction and operation of these facilities require land, which may lead to habitat disruption and changes in land use patterns. Careful site selection and design can help minimize these impacts. Environmental impact assessments (EIAs) are crucial tools in evaluating the potential ecological effects of WtE projects and identifying measures to mitigate them. Engaging with local communities and stakeholders during the planning process can also help address concerns and ensure that the project aligns with local environmental and social priorities.

The management of by-products, such as ash and sludge, poses additional environmental challenges. These residues may contain hazardous substances and require careful handling, treatment, and disposal to prevent environmental contamination. Technologies for ash stabilization and resource recovery are being developed to enhance the sustainability of WtE systems. For example, fly ash can be treated to remove heavy metals and used as a construction material, reducing the need for landfill disposal and supporting circular economy principles.

Climate change mitigation is a critical consideration in the deployment of WtE technologies. While these systems can contribute to renewable energy generation and reduce reliance on fossil fuels, their net impact on greenhouse gas emissions must be assessed. Some WtE processes produce carbon dioxide and other greenhouse gases, which can offset the climate benefits of renewable energy production. Life cycle assessments (LCAs) are essential tools for evaluating the overall carbon footprint of WtE systems and identifying opportunities for improvement. By optimizing process efficiencies and integrating carbon capture and storage technologies, WtE facilities can enhance their contributions to climate change mitigation.

Public perception and acceptance of WtE technologies are closely linked to their environmental performance. Concerns about emissions, odors, and potential health impacts can influence community attitudes and project approval. Transparent communication and stakeholder engagement are vital in building trust and support for WtE initiatives. Providing clear and accessible information about the environmental safeguards in place and the benefits of WtE technologies can help address misconceptions and foster positive relationships with local communities.

Regulatory frameworks and policy support are critical in addressing the environmental challenges associated with WtE technologies. Governments play a key role in establishing emissions standards, monitoring protocols, and incentives for sustainable waste management practices. By setting clear environmental performance criteria and providing financial support for research and development, policymakers can drive innovation and continuous improvement in the sector.

Technological advancements continue to enhance the environmental performance of WtE systems. Innovations in reactor design, materials science, and process optimization contribute to more efficient and cleaner operations. For example, improvements in gasification and pyrolysis technologies can reduce emissions and increase energy recovery efficiency, enhancing the overall sustainability of WtE projects. Ongoing research and collaboration among industry stakeholders, academia, and government agencies are essential in driving these advancements and ensuring that WtE technologies remain aligned with environmental priorities.

As societies transition to more sustainable waste management and energy systems, the environmental considerations and challenges of WtE technologies must be carefully navigated. By addressing these challenges through technological innovation, policy support, and stakeholder engagement, WtE systems can play a vital role in achieving sustainability goals. Emphasizing environmental stewardship and resource efficiency in the design and operation of WtE facilities can unlock their full potential as part of an integrated approach to waste management and energy production.

The journey towards a sustainable future requires a holistic understanding of the environmental implications of WtE technologies. By embracing a comprehensive approach that considers air and water quality, land use, climate impacts, and community engagement, stakeholders can ensure that these technologies contribute positively to environmental and social well-being. The continued evolution of WtE systems, guided by environmental considerations and challenges, will be instrumental in transforming waste into a valuable resource and fostering a more resilient and sustainable world.

Chapter 4: Circular Economy and Waste Reduction

Principles of the Circular Economy

The circular economy represents a transformative approach to economic development, one that is designed to benefit businesses, society, and the environment. In contrast to the traditional linear economy, which follows a 'take, make, dispose' model, the circular economy emphasizes resource efficiency, waste minimization, and the continual use of resources. At its core, the circular economy seeks to create closed-loop systems where waste is designed out of the process, products and materials are kept in use for as long as possible, and natural systems are regenerated.

One of the foundational principles of the circular economy is designing for longevity. This involves creating products that are durable, repairable, and upgradeable, extending their lifespan and reducing the need for new production. By prioritizing quality and durability, manufacturers can reduce the frequency of product replacement, thereby conserving resources and minimizing waste. This approach encourages innovation in product design, materials science, and engineering, fostering the development of products that are not only long-lasting but also adaptable to changing user needs and preferences.

Another key principle is the optimization of resource use. This involves maximizing the utility of materials and energy at every stage of the product lifecycle, from design and production to consumption and end-of-life management. Strategies such as resource recovery, remanufacturing, and recycling are integral to this principle, ensuring that materials are cycled back into the production process rather than being discarded. By optimizing resource use, businesses can reduce costs, improve efficiency, and enhance their environmental performance.

The circular economy also emphasizes the importance of regenerative systems. This principle recognizes that economic activities should contribute to the restoration and enhancement of natural ecosystems, rather than their degradation. Practices such as regenerative agriculture, sustainable forestry, and biodiversity conservation are examples of how economic activities can be aligned with ecological goals. By adopting regenerative practices, businesses can contribute to the health and resilience of the natural systems upon which they depend, supporting long-term sustainability and prosperity.

Collaboration and innovation are vital components of the circular economy. Achieving a circular economy requires cooperation across sectors, industries, and value chains. Businesses, governments, and civil society must work together to develop new business models, technologies, and policies that support circularity. Collaborative platforms and networks can facilitate knowledge sharing, innovation, and the scaling of successful circular practices. By working together, stakeholders can overcome barriers to circularity and unlock new opportunities for growth and development.

The transition to a circular economy also necessitates a shift in consumer behavior and mindset. Consumers play a crucial role in driving demand for circular products and services, and their choices can influence the adoption of circular practices. Educating consumers about the benefits of the circular economy, such as cost savings, environmental protection, and improved product quality, can encourage more sustainable consumption patterns. Initiatives such as product labeling, awareness campaigns, and incentives for sustainable consumption can support this shift, empowering consumers to make informed choices that align with circular principles.

Policy and regulatory frameworks are essential enablers of the circular economy. Governments have a critical role in creating the conditions for circular practices to thrive, through measures such as setting standards, providing incentives, and removing regulatory barriers. Policies that promote resource efficiency, waste reduction, and sustainable production and consumption can drive the adoption of circular practices across industries. Additionally, governments can support the development of circular infrastructure, such as recycling facilities and resource recovery systems, which are necessary for the effective implementation of circular models.

The circular economy offers significant economic, environmental, and social benefits. By reducing resource consumption and waste generation, the circular economy can contribute to environmental protection and climate change mitigation. It also offers economic opportunities through cost savings, job creation, and the development of new markets and business models. Socially, the circular economy can enhance quality of life by promoting sustainable consumption, improving product quality, and supporting community development.

Despite its potential, the transition to a circular economy is not without challenges. Barriers such as technological limitations, financial constraints, and resistance to change can impede progress. Overcoming these challenges requires concerted efforts from all stakeholders, including businesses, governments, and consumers. Investment in research and development, capacity building, and education is crucial to advancing circular practices and overcoming these barriers.

The principles of the circular economy provide a framework for rethinking the way we produce, consume, and manage resources. By embracing these principles, businesses and societies can create a more sustainable and resilient future, where economic growth is decoupled from resource consumption and environmental impact. As the global community seeks solutions to pressing challenges such as climate change, resource scarcity, and waste, the circular economy stands as a promising pathway towards a more sustainable and equitable world.

In conclusion, the circular economy represents a paradigm shift in how we view and interact with our resources. By focusing on longevity, resource optimization, regeneration, collaboration, and innovation, the circular economy offers a blueprint for sustainable development that benefits both people and the planet. As we continue to explore and implement circular practices, we pave the way for a future where resources are used wisely, waste is minimized, and natural systems are respected and restored. The journey towards a circular economy is both a challenge and an opportunity, one that requires commitment, creativity, and collaboration from all sectors of society.

Designing Products for Longevity and Reuse

Designing products with longevity and reuse in mind is pivotal in fostering a sustainable future. This approach not only conserves resources but also minimizes waste, aligning with the principles of a circular economy. By prioritizing durability, repairability, and adaptability, manufacturers can create products that stand the test of time and evolve with changing consumer needs.

Durability is a cornerstone of designing for longevity. Products that are built to last reduce the frequency of replacement and the demand for new resources. This begins with the selection of high-quality materials that can withstand wear and tear. Engineers and designers must consider the entire lifecycle of a product, ensuring that its components endure various stresses and conditions. For instance, stainless steel, hardwood, and reinforced plastics are often chosen for their resilience in demanding environments. By opting for robust materials and construction methods, manufacturers can ensure that their products remain functional and aesthetically pleasing for years.

Repairability is another critical aspect of product design that extends its lifespan. In a world where technology and consumer preferences evolve rapidly, the ability to repair and upgrade products is increasingly important. Designing products with modularity in mind allows for easy replacement of individual parts rather than discarding the entire item. This approach not only extends the product's life but also empowers consumers to maintain and customize their possessions. Providing consumers with access to spare parts, repair manuals, and support services is essential in facilitating repairability. By fostering a culture of repair, manufacturers can reduce waste and promote sustainable consumption.

Adaptability is equally important in designing products for longevity. Products that can be easily adapted or repurposed for different uses or environments offer greater value and reduce the need for new purchases. For example, furniture that can be reconfigured to suit different spaces or needs, or electronics that can be upgraded with new features, exemplify adaptability in design. This flexibility not only enhances the product's utility but also contributes to consumer satisfaction and brand loyalty.

Incorporating timeless design and aesthetics plays a significant role in ensuring that products remain desirable over time. Trends come and go, but classic designs have enduring appeal. By focusing on simplicity, functionality, and elegance, designers can create products that transcend short-lived fads and remain relevant to consumers across generations. This approach not only enhances the product's longevity but also reduces the environmental impact of frequent style changes and disposability.

The use of sustainable materials is integral to designing products for longevity and reuse. By selecting materials that are renewable, recyclable, or biodegradable, manufacturers can reduce the environmental footprint of their products. For instance, using recycled metals, certified sustainable wood, and biodegradable plastics can contribute to resource conservation and waste reduction. Additionally, designing products with the end-of-life phase in mind ensures that materials can be recovered and reintegrated into the production cycle, supporting circularity and resource efficiency.

Engaging consumers in the process of designing for longevity and reuse is crucial for success. Educating consumers about the benefits of durable and repairable products can shift preferences and behaviors toward more sustainable choices. Providing information on how to care for and maintain products can empower consumers to extend their lifespan and maximize their value. Furthermore, offering incentives for returning or recycling products can facilitate reuse and resource recovery, closing the loop in the product lifecycle.

Collaboration among designers, manufacturers, and stakeholders is essential in advancing the principles of longevity and reuse. By working together, stakeholders can share knowledge, resources, and best practices to develop innovative solutions that enhance product durability and sustainability. Industry standards and certifications can also play a role in promoting best practices and ensuring accountability. By fostering a collaborative ecosystem, the industry can drive continuous improvement and innovation in product design.

The integration of technology and smart design features can further enhance product longevity and adaptability. For example, incorporating sensors and connectivity into products can enable predictive maintenance, alerting users to potential issues before they become critical. Smart features can also facilitate customization and adaptation, allowing products to evolve with changing needs and preferences. By leveraging technology, designers can create products that are not only durable but also intelligent and responsive.

Economic considerations also influence the design of products for longevity and reuse. While designing for durability may involve higher upfront costs, the long-term benefits, such as reduced resource consumption, waste management expenses, and consumer loyalty, can outweigh these initial investments. Manufacturers can capture value by offering extended warranties, maintenance services, and product leasing models that align with the principles of longevity and reuse. These models not only provide revenue streams but also strengthen customer relationships and brand reputation.

The journey toward designing products for longevity and reuse requires a shift in mindset and practices. By embracing a holistic approach that considers the entire lifecycle of a product, manufacturers can create solutions that benefit both people and the planet. As the global community seeks to address pressing environmental challenges and resource constraints, designing for longevity and reuse offers a pathway to a more sustainable and resilient future.

In the quest for sustainability, the principles of durability, repairability, adaptability, and collaboration converge to redefine how products are conceived, manufactured, and consumed. By focusing on longevity and reuse, designers and manufacturers can contribute to a world where resources are used wisely, waste is minimized, and products are valued for their enduring quality and utility. As we move forward, the commitment to designing products for longevity and reuse will serve as a guiding light, illuminating the path to a circular and sustainable economy.

Implementing Circular Business Models

Implementing circular business models is a transformative strategy that enables companies to thrive in an environment increasingly focused on sustainability. These models move away from the traditional linear approach of 'take, make, dispose' and embrace a more regenerative system where resources are reused, materials are recycled, and products are designed with their entire lifecycle in mind. By integrating circular principles, businesses can unlock new opportunities for innovation, reduce costs, and enhance their competitive advantage.

A critical aspect of circular business models is the shift from ownership to access. This paradigm encourages companies to offer products as a service rather than a one-time purchase. For instance, instead of selling equipment outright, businesses can lease or rent their products, retaining ownership and responsibility for maintenance and eventual recycling. This approach not only reduces waste but also fosters ongoing relationships with customers, providing continuous revenue streams and opportunities for upselling and cross-selling.

Designing products for longevity and modularity is another essential element of circular business models. By creating products that are durable, repairable, and upgradeable, companies can extend their useful life and reduce the need for constant replacement. Modularity allows for easy disassembly and reconfiguration, enabling components to be updated or replaced as needed. This not only conserves resources but also aligns with the growing consumer demand for sustainable and high-quality products.

Resource recovery and recycling are integral components of circular business practices. Companies can implement systems to collect and process end-of-life products, reclaim valuable materials, and reintegrate them into the production cycle. This approach not only minimizes waste but also reduces reliance on virgin resources, decreasing environmental impact and enhancing supply chain resilience. Collaborations with recycling facilities, waste management companies, and other stakeholders are crucial to developing efficient recovery systems that support circularity.

Innovative business models also focus on creating value from by-products and waste streams. By identifying secondary markets or developing new applications for waste materials, companies can transform potential liabilities into valuable assets. For example, food manufacturers can convert organic waste into biogas or animal feed, while textile companies might repurpose fabric scraps into insulation materials. These strategies not only generate additional revenue but also contribute to resource efficiency and waste reduction.

Digital technologies play a crucial role in enabling circular business models. The integration of IoT, blockchain, and data analytics can enhance transparency, traceability, and efficiency throughout the value chain. IoT devices can monitor product performance and usage, providing insights into maintenance needs and facilitating predictive maintenance. Blockchain technology can ensure the authenticity and provenance of materials, supporting closed-loop supply chains and fostering consumer trust. Data analytics can identify patterns and opportunities for optimization, driving continuous improvement and innovation.

The transition to circular business models requires a cultural shift within organizations. Leadership commitment and employee engagement are vital to embedding circular principles into corporate strategy and operations. Training programs and workshops can help build awareness and understanding of circular practices, empowering employees to identify opportunities for improvement and contribute to the company's sustainability goals. Cultivating a culture of innovation and collaboration encourages cross-functional teams to explore new ideas and solutions that support circularity.

Collaboration across industries and sectors is essential for scaling circular business models. By partnering with suppliers, customers, and other stakeholders, companies can share resources, knowledge, and best practices to overcome barriers and drive systemic change. Industry associations and networks can facilitate collaboration, providing platforms for dialogue and exchange that accelerate the adoption of circular practices. Public-private partnerships can also play a crucial role in developing infrastructure, policies, and incentives that support circular business models.

Engaging consumers is a critical component of implementing circular business models. Educating and informing customers about the benefits of circular products and services can shift preferences and behaviors toward more sustainable choices. Transparent communication about product lifecycles, resource use, and environmental impact builds trust and fosters loyalty. Companies can also involve consumers in the circular process by offering take-back schemes, repair services, and incentives for returning or recycling products.

Regulatory frameworks and policy support are crucial enablers of circular business models. Governments can create favorable conditions for circularity by establishing standards, providing incentives, and removing regulatory barriers. Policies that promote resource efficiency, waste reduction, and sustainable production and consumption can accelerate the adoption of circular practices across industries. Additionally, governments can support the development of circular infrastructure, such as recycling facilities and resource recovery systems, which are necessary for the effective implementation of circular models.

The economic benefits of circular business models are significant. By reducing resource consumption and waste generation, companies can achieve cost savings, improve efficiency, and enhance their environmental performance. Circular practices can also open new markets and revenue streams, driving innovation and competitiveness. Socially, circular business models contribute to job creation, community development, and improved quality of life by promoting sustainable consumption and production patterns.

The journey toward implementing circular business models is both a challenge and an opportunity. By embracing circular principles, companies can transform their operations, enhance their resilience, and contribute to a more sustainable and equitable future. As the global community seeks solutions to pressing challenges such as climate change, resource scarcity, and waste, circular business models offer a promising pathway toward a more sustainable and resilient global economy.

In the quest for sustainability, the commitment to circular business practices will serve as a guiding light, illuminating the path to a circular and sustainable economy. Through innovation, collaboration, and a focus on value creation, businesses can redefine success and drive positive change for both people and the planet. As we move forward, the implementation of circular business models will be instrumental in shaping a world where resources are used wisely, waste is minimized, and economic prosperity is aligned with environmental stewardship.

Case Studies of Successful Circular Initiatives

Throughout the world, innovative companies and organizations are leading the way in implementing circular economy principles, transforming waste into valuable resources and redefining sustainability in their industries. These case studies of successful circular initiatives provide compelling examples of how circular practices can be effectively integrated into business models, yielding economic, environmental, and social benefits.

One exemplary case is that of a global furniture retailer that has embraced circular design and resource recovery. This company has committed to producing all its products using renewable or recycled materials by a specific target year. To achieve this, it has implemented a take-back program, allowing customers to return used furniture for refurbishment and resale. This initiative not only extends the life of products but also reduces the need for virgin materials. The company has invested in designing modular furniture that can be easily disassembled, repaired, and customized, thus enhancing longevity and adaptability. By fostering a culture of sustainability among its customers and employees, the retailer has successfully integrated circular practices into its operations, setting a new standard for the industry.

In the fashion sector, a renowned clothing brand has made significant strides in circularity through its innovative recycling program. Recognizing the environmental impact of textile waste, the brand has developed a closed-loop system that collects used garments from customers and recycles them into new products. This initiative involves collaboration with recycling partners and investment in advanced sorting and processing technologies. The brand has also focused on sustainable design, creating garments that are durable, timeless, and made from eco-friendly materials. By engaging consumers through transparent communication and incentivizing participation in the recycling program, the brand has not only reduced its environmental footprint but also strengthened its relationship with environmentally conscious customers.

The electronics industry offers another inspirational example with a leading tech company that has pioneered circular practices in its product lifecycle management. This company has adopted a holistic approach to sustainability, encompassing design, production, use, and end-of-life. It produces devices with modular components that are easy to upgrade and repair, reducing electronic waste and extending product life. The company has also implemented a robust trade-in program, encouraging customers to return old devices for recycling or refurbishment. These efforts are supported by a comprehensive supply chain strategy that prioritizes recycled materials and energy-efficient manufacturing processes. The tech company's commitment to circularity has not only enhanced its brand reputation but also driven innovation and cost savings.

In the automotive industry, a leading car manufacturer has embraced circular economy principles to reduce its environmental impact and enhance resource efficiency. This company has focused on designing vehicles with recyclable materials, energy-efficient technologies, and modular components. It has also developed a take-back program for end-of-life vehicles, ensuring that materials such as metals, plastics, and batteries are recovered and reused in new cars. By integrating circular practices into its production and value chain, the manufacturer has achieved significant reductions in waste and emissions, demonstrating the potential for circularity in a traditionally resource-intensive industry.

The food and agriculture sector also showcases successful circular initiatives, as seen in the efforts of an innovative agricultural cooperative. This cooperative has implemented regenerative farming practices that enhance soil health, increase biodiversity, and reduce chemical inputs. It has also developed a closed-loop system for managing organic waste, converting it into compost and biogas. These initiatives have not only improved the environmental sustainability of the cooperative's operations but also increased resilience and productivity. By engaging with local communities and stakeholders, the cooperative has fostered a shared commitment to sustainability and circularity, creating economic and social value.

In the construction industry, a pioneering company has demonstrated the potential of circular practices through its sustainable building projects. This company has adopted a circular approach to construction, using prefabricated components, recycled materials, and energy-efficient designs. It has also implemented deconstruction practices that allow for the recovery and reuse of building materials at the end of a building's life. By integrating circularity into its construction processes, the company has reduced waste, lowered costs, and created healthier, more sustainable buildings. Its projects serve as models for the industry, illustrating the feasibility and benefits of circular construction practices.

Another noteworthy example is a city that has embraced circular economy principles to transform its waste management system. Faced with increasing waste and resource challenges, the city has developed an integrated waste management strategy that prioritizes recycling, composting, and resource recovery. This approach involves collaboration with local businesses, residents, and waste management companies to create a circular ecosystem that minimizes waste and maximizes resource use. The city has also invested in education and outreach programs to engage the community and promote sustainable behaviors. These efforts have resulted in significant reductions in waste sent to landfill and increased resource recovery rates, positioning the city as a leader in urban sustainability.

These case studies highlight the diverse ways in which circular economy principles can be successfully implemented across different sectors and contexts. They demonstrate that circular initiatives are not only feasible but also beneficial, offering tangible advantages for businesses, communities, and the environment. The success of these initiatives is often driven by a combination of innovation, collaboration, and a commitment to sustainability. By learning from these examples, other organizations and stakeholders can be inspired to adopt and adapt circular practices to their unique circumstances.

The transition to a circular economy requires a shift in mindset and practices, but the rewards are significant. By embracing circularity, organizations can enhance their resilience, reduce their environmental impact, and create new value for themselves and their stakeholders. As more companies and communities embark on this journey, the cumulative impact of circular initiatives will contribute to a more sustainable and equitable world, where resources are used wisely, waste is minimized, and economic prosperity is aligned with environmental stewardship. Through continued innovation and collaboration, the vision of a circular economy can be realized, offering a brighter future for current and future generations.

Measuring the Impact of Circular Practices

Understanding the impact of circular practices is essential for businesses and organizations aiming to transition towards sustainable models. Measuring the effects of these practices not only validates their efficacy but also informs strategy and improvements. To ensure comprehensive assessment, a structured approach combining quantitative and qualitative metrics is necessary. This holistic view captures the multifaceted benefits of circularity, ranging from environmental improvements to economic gains and social advancements.

The first step in measuring circular practices is identifying relevant indicators. Environmental metrics often take precedence, given their critical role in sustainability. Tracking reductions in resource consumption, such as energy, water, and raw materials, provides insight into the efficiency gains achieved through circular methods. Likewise, monitoring waste generation and disposal gives a direct measure of how well a company or initiative is performing in minimizing waste. These indicators are usually quantified through Life Cycle Assessments (LCAs), which evaluate the environmental impacts of a product or process across its entire lifecycle.

Incorporating economic metrics is equally important in assessing the impact of circular practices. Cost savings from reduced material usage, waste management, and energy consumption often serve as compelling arguments for the adoption of circular models. Additionally, circular practices can open new revenue streams through the sale of recycled materials, refurbished products, or services such as leasing. Tracking these financial metrics can demonstrate the economic viability and potential profitability of circular initiatives, providing a strong business case for their implementation.

Social impacts, though often less tangible, are a key component of measuring circular practices. Job creation in areas such as recycling, repair, and remanufacturing highlights the potential for circular economies to support employment. Moreover, improvements in community well-being and engagement, driven by sustainable practices and local collaborations, underscore the social benefits of circularity. Surveys, interviews, and community feedback can be used to gather qualitative data on these social dimensions, complementing the quantitative metrics.

Implementing a robust data collection system is crucial for accurately measuring the impact of circular practices. This involves establishing clear methodologies and protocols for data gathering, ensuring consistency and reliability of information. Companies can leverage technology to streamline data collection and analysis, using tools such as software platforms and IoT devices to monitor resource flows and track performance in real-time. This technology-driven approach not only enhances accuracy but also enables dynamic reporting and decision-making.

Benchmarking against industry standards and best practices provides context for evaluating circular initiatives. By comparing performance with peers and industry leaders, organizations can identify areas for improvement and set realistic targets. This competitive analysis also fosters a culture of continuous improvement and innovation, encouraging companies to push the boundaries of what is possible within a circular framework.

Transparency and communication play a vital role in the measurement process. Sharing results with stakeholders, including employees, customers, and investors, builds trust and accountability. Transparent reporting on circular practices and their impacts demonstrates a company's commitment to sustainability and can enhance its reputation and brand value. Furthermore, engaging stakeholders in the measurement process can yield valuable insights and foster collaborative efforts to drive further progress.

Challenges in measuring the impact of circular practices do exist, and companies must be prepared to address them. The complexity of supply chains, variability in data quality, and lack of standardized metrics can hinder accurate assessment. To overcome these obstacles, organizations must invest in capacity building and develop expertise in sustainability measurement and reporting. Collaboration with industry groups, NGOs, and academic institutions can also support the development of standardized frameworks and methodologies, facilitating more consistent and comparable assessments.

The feedback loop created by measuring the impact of circular practices is essential for driving continuous improvement. By analyzing results and identifying areas for enhancement, companies can refine their strategies and optimize their circular initiatives. This iterative process ensures that circular practices remain effective and relevant, adapting to changing circumstances and advancing towards sustainability goals.

Measuring the impact of circular practices is not merely a retrospective exercise; it is a proactive approach to shaping the future of business and society. By understanding the benefits and challenges of circular models, organizations can make informed decisions that align with their values and objectives. The insights gained from measurement drive innovation, enhance resilience, and contribute to a more sustainable and equitable world.

As the global community increasingly recognizes the importance of sustainability, the ability to measure and demonstrate the impact of circular practices becomes a competitive advantage. Companies that effectively assess and communicate their circular achievements are better positioned to capture market opportunities, attract investment, and build strong stakeholder relationships. By committing to rigorous measurement and transparent reporting, businesses can lead the way in creating a circular economy that benefits all.

Ultimately, measuring the impact of circular practices is about more than just data and metrics; it is about understanding the broader implications of our actions and making choices that support a sustainable future. Through comprehensive assessment and continuous improvement, we can harness the power of circularity to transform industries and create lasting positive change. The journey towards a circular economy is complex, but with the right tools and commitment, it is a journey that holds immense promise and potential for a brighter tomorrow.

Chapter 5: Innovative Recycling Techniques

Advances in Plastic Recycling Technologies

Plastic recycling technologies have seen significant advancements as the global community grapples with the environmental challenges posed by plastic waste. These innovations are critical in reducing the dependency on virgin plastic production and mitigating the ecological footprint of plastic pollution. With increasing consumer awareness and regulatory pressures, industries are exploring cutting-edge technologies that enhance the efficiency and effectiveness of recycling processes.

Mechanical recycling remains one of the most widely used methods for processing plastic waste. This technique involves sorting, cleaning, shredding, and melting plastics to create new products. Recent innovations in mechanical recycling focus on improving the sorting process using advanced technologies such as near-infrared (NIR) spectroscopy and AI-driven sorting systems. These technologies enable more precise separation of different types of plastics based on their chemical composition and color, resulting in higher quality recyclates and reducing contamination in the recycling stream.

Chemical recycling, also known as feedstock recycling, is gaining traction as a promising alternative to mechanical recycling. This process breaks down plastic polymers into their monomers or other valuable chemicals using heat, solvents, or catalysts. Chemical recycling offers the advantage of processing mixed or contaminated plastics that are challenging to recycle mechanically. Technologies such as pyrolysis, depolymerization, and solvolysis are at the forefront of this field, converting plastic waste into feedstock for new plastic production or other industrial applications. These processes not only contribute to a circular economy but also offer the potential to upcycle low-value plastics into high-quality materials.

Biological recycling is an emerging area that leverages microorganisms and enzymes to degrade plastics into simpler compounds. This method holds promise for addressing the challenges associated with traditional recycling techniques, such as energy consumption and limited material recovery. Researchers are exploring the potential of bacteria and fungi that can metabolize plastics, offering a sustainable and eco-friendly approach to recycling. Enzymatic recycling, in particular, has shown potential for breaking down PET plastics into their building blocks, which can then be reused to produce new PET products. Although still in the developmental stage, biological recycling represents a frontier in the quest for sustainable plastic management.

Innovations in additive manufacturing, also known as 3D printing, are also contributing to advancements in plastic recycling. This technology allows for the direct conversion of recycled plastics into new products with minimal processing. By utilizing recycled filaments in 3D printing, manufacturers can create customized and complex products while minimizing waste. This approach not only conserves resources but also encourages localized production and reduces transportation emissions. The integration of recycled materials into 3D printing is paving the way for a more sustainable manufacturing paradigm.

Closed-loop recycling systems are being developed to ensure that plastic products are recycled back into the same products or similar applications. This approach involves designing products with recyclability in mind and establishing collection and recycling infrastructure to facilitate the return of used products. Companies are increasingly adopting closed-loop systems to meet sustainability goals and regulatory requirements. By closing the loop on plastic waste, these systems help maintain the value of materials within the economy while reducing the demand for virgin resources.

Digital technologies are playing a crucial role in enhancing the efficiency and traceability of plastic recycling. Blockchain technology, for instance, is being used to track the movement of plastic waste through the supply chain, ensuring transparency and accountability. Digital platforms are also enabling better coordination between stakeholders, facilitating the exchange of recycled materials and optimizing logistics. These innovations are instrumental in creating a more connected and efficient recycling ecosystem.

Consumer participation is vital for the success of plastic recycling technologies. Engaging consumers through education and awareness campaigns can drive behavior change and increase recycling rates. Initiatives such as deposit return schemes, rewards for recycling, and clear labeling of recyclable materials can incentivize consumers to participate actively in recycling efforts. By fostering a culture of responsibility and sustainability, individuals can contribute significantly to the reduction of plastic waste.

Collaboration across sectors and industries is essential for advancing plastic recycling technologies. Partnerships between manufacturers, recyclers, academia, and governments can accelerate research and development efforts and facilitate the implementation of innovative solutions. Public-private partnerships, in particular, can play a pivotal role in scaling up recycling infrastructure and creating supportive policy environments. By working together, stakeholders can overcome technical and economic barriers to recycling and drive systemic change.

Challenges remain in the widespread adoption of advanced plastic recycling technologies. High costs, technical limitations, and market barriers can hinder the deployment of new solutions. However, continued investment in research and development, along with supportive policies and incentives, can address these challenges and unlock the potential of these technologies. By prioritizing sustainability and innovation, industries can pave the way for a more resilient and circular plastic economy.

The progress in plastic recycling technologies marks a significant step towards a more sustainable future. As these technologies continue to evolve, they offer the potential to transform the way plastic waste is managed and utilized. By embracing innovation and collaboration, we can create a world where plastics are not a burden but a valuable resource, contributing to a cleaner and healthier planet. The journey towards advanced plastic recycling is ongoing, and with each advancement, we move closer to a sustainable and circular economy.

Chemical Recycling: Opportunities and Challenges

Chemical recycling is emerging as a transformative approach in the quest to manage plastic waste sustainably. Unlike traditional mechanical recycling, which primarily deals with thermoplastics, chemical recycling breaks down polymers into monomers or other valuable chemicals, offering a broader scope for recycling diverse types of plastics. This process presents numerous opportunities but also brings its own set of challenges that must be addressed for widespread adoption.

Opportunities within chemical recycling are vast, with the potential to significantly impact environmental sustainability. By converting mixed and contaminated plastics into valuable materials, chemical recycling can tackle the challenge posed by plastic types that mechanical methods struggle to process. This capability not only expands the range of recyclable materials but also reduces the volume of waste ending up in landfills or incinerators, thereby mitigating environmental pollution.

One of the most promising aspects of chemical recycling is its ability to produce high-quality recycled materials. Unlike mechanical recycling, which can degrade the quality of plastics over successive cycles, chemical recycling allows for the recovery of virgin-quality monomers. This process ensures that the resulting materials maintain their integrity and performance, making them suitable for high-value applications, including food-grade packaging and medical products. By providing materials that meet stringent quality standards, chemical recycling can help close the loop on plastic waste and create a truly circular economy.

From an economic perspective, chemical recycling can open new revenue streams and market opportunities. The value of recovered chemicals and monomers can offset the costs associated with the recycling process, making it an economically viable option for businesses. Moreover, the adoption of chemical recycling technologies can enhance a company's sustainability credentials, appealing to environmentally conscious consumers and investors. This alignment with sustainable development goals can drive competitive advantage and long-term growth.

Despite its potential, chemical recycling faces several challenges that must be overcome to realize its full benefits. One of the primary obstacles is the high energy consumption associated with some chemical recycling processes. Techniques such as pyrolysis and gasification require significant energy inputs to break down plastics, which can offset the environmental benefits of recycling. Advancements in process efficiency and energy recovery are necessary to make chemical recycling more sustainable and economically feasible.

Another challenge lies in the complexity of scaling up chemical recycling technologies. Many of these processes are still in the developmental or pilot stages, requiring investment and innovation to reach commercial viability. Establishing the necessary infrastructure, from collection and sorting systems to processing facilities, presents logistical and financial hurdles. Collaboration between government, industry, and academia is crucial to driving research and development efforts, securing funding, and creating supportive policy frameworks.

The regulatory landscape also poses challenges for chemical recycling. Ensuring compliance with environmental and safety standards is critical, particularly when producing materials intended for sensitive applications like food packaging. Developing clear regulations and guidelines will be essential to facilitate the growth of chemical recycling while safeguarding public health and the environment.

Consumer perception and engagement are additional factors that influence the success of chemical recycling initiatives. Educating the public about the benefits and safety of chemically recycled products can help build trust and acceptance. Transparent communication about the processes, materials, and impacts of chemical recycling will be key to fostering consumer confidence and encouraging participation in recycling programs.

Addressing feedstock variability is another challenge faced by chemical recycling technologies. The diverse composition of plastic waste streams can affect process efficiency and output quality. Developing adaptable technologies that can handle a wide range of feedstock types and qualities is essential for maximizing the potential of chemical recycling. Innovations in sorting and preprocessing technologies can enhance feedstock preparation, ensuring consistent and high-quality input for chemical recycling processes.

The potential for chemical recycling to contribute to a circular economy is significant, but realizing this potential requires a concerted effort from all stakeholders. Investment in research and development, supportive policies, and public-private partnerships are critical to overcoming the challenges and scaling up chemical recycling technologies. By fostering innovation and collaboration, the industry can develop solutions that enhance process efficiency, reduce costs, and improve environmental outcomes.

Chemical recycling represents a promising frontier in waste management and resource recovery. Its ability to handle complex and contaminated plastics, produce high-quality materials, and support circular economy goals makes it an attractive option for addressing the global plastic waste crisis. While challenges remain, the opportunities presented by chemical recycling are too significant to ignore. By advancing this technology and integrating it into broader waste management strategies, we can move closer to a sustainable future where plastics are part of a closed-loop system, contributing to environmental stewardship and economic prosperity.

The Rise of E-Waste Recycling Solutions

Electronic waste, or e-waste, has rapidly emerged as one of the fastest-growing waste streams in the world, fueled by the constant evolution of technology and the consumer demand for the latest devices. As a result, e-waste recycling solutions have gained significant attention, offering a way to mitigate the environmental impact of discarded electronics while recovering valuable materials. This chapter delves into the rise of e-waste recycling, exploring the innovative solutions being developed and implemented to address this pressing issue.

The sheer scale of e-waste generation presents both a challenge and an opportunity. Millions of tons of electronic devices are discarded each year, ranging from smartphones and laptops to household appliances and industrial equipment. These items often contain hazardous materials, such as lead, mercury, and cadmium, which can pose serious environmental and health risks if not properly managed. At the same time, e-waste is a rich source of valuable resources, including precious metals like gold, silver, and platinum, as well as rare earth elements. Efficient recycling solutions can not only prevent environmental contamination but also recover these resources for reuse, reducing the need for virgin materials and supporting a circular economy.

One of the key advancements in e-waste recycling is the development of more sophisticated sorting and dismantling technologies. Automated systems equipped with robotics and artificial intelligence are being used to disassemble devices, separating components and materials with precision and efficiency. These technologies can handle complex products, such as smartphones and circuit boards, which contain a variety of materials tightly integrated within compact designs. By improving the accuracy and speed of sorting processes, these technologies enhance the recovery of valuable materials and reduce contamination, resulting in higher-quality recyclates.

Hydrometallurgical and pyrometallurgical processes are among the most common methods for recovering metals from e-waste. Hydrometallurgy involves the use of aqueous solutions to dissolve metals, which are then extracted through various chemical reactions. This method is particularly effective for recovering precious metals and is often employed for processing circuit boards. Pyrometallurgy, on the other hand, uses high temperatures to smelt metals, separating them from other materials. While both processes have their advantages, they also pose environmental challenges, such as the generation of toxic emissions and waste. Advances in these technologies are focusing on improving efficiency and reducing environmental impact, such as through the development of closed-loop systems that capture emissions and recycle process chemicals.

An emerging area of e-waste recycling is the use of biotechnological methods, where microorganisms and enzymes are employed to recover metals from electronic waste. This approach, known as bioleaching, offers a more environmentally friendly alternative to traditional chemical processes. Certain bacteria and fungi have the ability to solubilize metals, making them accessible for recovery. This method can be particularly useful for extracting metals from low-grade ores and waste streams that are difficult to process using conventional techniques. Although still in the research phase, biotechnological solutions hold promise for sustainable e-waste recycling in the future.

The concept of urban mining is gaining traction as a strategy to recover valuable resources from e-waste. Urban mining refers to the extraction of metals and other materials from existing products and waste, rather than from traditional mining operations. By tapping into the "mines" of urban areas, such as landfills and electronic waste streams, urban mining can help meet the demand for raw materials while reducing the environmental impact associated with conventional mining. This approach underscores the importance of e-waste recycling as a means of resource recovery and sustainable development.

Extended producer responsibility (EPR) policies are playing a crucial role in promoting e-waste recycling solutions. EPR holds manufacturers accountable for the end-of-life management of their products, incentivizing them to design for recyclability and establish take-back programs. These policies encourage the development of infrastructure and technologies for e-waste collection, processing, and recycling, fostering a culture of responsibility and sustainability within the electronics industry. Collaboration between governments, manufacturers, and recyclers is essential to ensure the effective implementation of EPR and the growth of e-waste recycling solutions.

Consumer awareness and participation are vital components of successful e-waste recycling initiatives. Educating the public about the importance of recycling electronics and the potential environmental and economic benefits can drive behavior change and increase recycling rates. Initiatives such as e-waste collection events, drop-off centers, and incentives for recycling can encourage consumers to dispose of their devices responsibly. By fostering a culture of sustainability, individuals can play an active role in reducing e-waste and supporting the transition to a circular economy.

Challenges remain in the widespread adoption of e-waste recycling solutions, including the complexity of electronic products, the presence of hazardous materials, and the economic viability of recycling processes. However, continued innovation and investment in research and development are driving progress in overcoming these obstacles. The development of more efficient and environmentally friendly recycling technologies, along with supportive policies and consumer engagement, will be key to unlocking the full potential of e-waste recycling.

The rise of e-waste recycling solutions marks a significant step towards addressing the global challenge of electronic waste. By harnessing the power of innovation and collaboration, we can create a more sustainable future where electronic products are part of a closed-loop system, contributing to resource conservation and environmental stewardship. As we continue to advance e-waste recycling technologies and practices, we move closer to a world where waste is minimized, resources are maximized, and economic prosperity is aligned with ecological responsibility.

Closing the Loop: Textile and Clothing Recycling

The fashion industry, with its rapid cycles and ever-changing trends, has long been associated with significant environmental impacts, from resource consumption to waste generation. As awareness of these effects grows, so does the interest in closing the loop through textile and clothing recycling. This chapter delves into the innovative solutions and practices that are transforming the way we manage textile waste, creating a more sustainable future for fashion.

In the past, the journey of a garment often ended in a landfill, with textiles accounting for a substantial portion of municipal solid waste. However, a shift is underway as stakeholders across the industry seek to embrace circular economy principles. Textile recycling encompasses a range of processes aimed at reusing, repurposing, and recycling fibers from discarded clothing and textiles, thereby minimizing waste and conserving resources.

Mechanical recycling has long been the cornerstone of textile recycling efforts. This process involves shredding fabrics into fibers that can be spun into yarns and woven into new textiles. While effective, mechanical recycling can pose challenges, such as fiber degradation, which limits the quality and application of recycled materials. Recent advancements in this field focus on improving fiber recovery and quality through innovative technologies and techniques. For example, advanced sorting systems using spectroscopic analysis can identify and separate different fiber types with accuracy, ensuring higher-quality recyclates.

Chemical recycling presents a promising alternative, particularly for complex textiles that are difficult to process mechanically. This method involves breaking down fibers into their chemical components, which can then be used to produce new fibers or other materials. Technologies such as depolymerization and solvent-based recycling are gaining traction, offering the potential to recycle textiles into virgin-quality fibers. These processes not only expand the range of recyclable materials but also allow for the production of high-performance textiles suitable for various applications.

Innovations in textile recycling are not limited to traditional fibers like cotton and polyester. Researchers are exploring the potential of recycling other materials, such as nylon and elastane, which are prevalent in performance and activewear. By developing processes that can effectively recycle these materials, the industry can further close the loop on textile waste and reduce its environmental footprint.

Design for circularity is an essential component of closing the loop in the fashion industry. By designing products with recyclability in mind, manufacturers can facilitate the recycling process and enhance material recovery. This involves selecting materials that are easily recyclable, using designs that allow for easy disassembly, and minimizing the use of mixed materials that complicate recycling. Design for circularity not only supports recycling efforts but also encourages innovation and creativity in sustainable fashion.

Take-back and collection programs are critical for ensuring that textiles reach recycling facilities rather than landfills. Many brands and retailers are implementing take-back schemes, offering consumers incentives to return their used garments. These programs provide a steady supply of feedstock for recycling processes and foster a sense of responsibility among consumers. Collaboration between brands, retailers, and recycling companies can enhance the efficiency and effectiveness of these programs, ensuring that textiles are collected and processed in a sustainable manner.

Consumer engagement and education play a pivotal role in the success of textile recycling initiatives. By raising awareness about the environmental impact of fashion and the importance of recycling, brands can encourage consumers to make more sustainable choices. Initiatives such as educational campaigns, clear labeling of recyclable products, and transparency about recycling processes can empower consumers to participate actively in the circular economy. As consumers become more informed and engaged, they can drive demand for sustainable products and practices within the industry.

The rise of digital technologies is facilitating the tracking and management of textile waste, making it easier to close the loop. Blockchain technology, for example, can provide transparency and traceability throughout the supply chain, ensuring that textiles are recycled responsibly. Digital platforms can also connect consumers with recycling services, streamlining the process of returning and recycling garments. These technologies not only enhance the efficiency of recycling systems but also build trust and accountability among stakeholders.

Despite the progress being made, challenges remain in the widespread adoption of textile recycling solutions. Economic barriers, such as the cost of recycling compared to virgin material production, can hinder investment and growth in the sector. Technical challenges, including the recycling of blended fabrics and garments with complex constructions, require ongoing research and innovation. To overcome these obstacles, collaboration and investment in research and development are essential. Public-private partnerships, along with supportive policies and incentives, can drive the advancement of textile recycling technologies and practices.

Closing the loop in the fashion industry is not just about recycling; it's about reimagining the entire lifecycle of textiles and clothing. By embracing circular economy principles, stakeholders can create a more sustainable and resilient industry that minimizes waste and maximizes resource efficiency. As the industry continues to innovate and adapt, textile recycling offers a pathway to a future where fashion is not only stylish but also sustainable.

The journey towards closing the loop in textile and clothing recycling is ongoing, but the progress made thus far is promising. By harnessing the power of innovation and collaboration, the fashion industry can transition towards a circular model that benefits both the environment and the economy. With each advancement, we move closer to a world where textiles are part of a closed-loop system, contributing to a sustainable and prosperous future for all.